BETTER BUSINESS BUREAU®

Insider's Guide to Success

Buying a Home

The Better Business Bureau
with Alice LaPlante

D0520097

thePlanningshop™

Palo Alto, California

Northern Plains Public Library
Ault Colorado

Better Business Bureau Buying a Home: Insider's Guide to Success
©2007 by Rhonda Abrams. Published by The Planning Shop™

All rights reserved. No part of this publication may be reproduced, transmitted, stored in an information retrieval system, or used in any form or by any means, graphic, electronic, mechanical, photocopying, recording, or otherwise, without the prior written permission of the publisher.

Better Business Bureau, BBB and the BBB torch logo are federally registered service marks owned by the Council of Better Business Bureaus, Inc. These marks may be used, with certain restrictions, by Better Business Bureaus and eligible companies participating in Better Business Bureau programs under a license agreement.

ISBN 13: 978-1-933895-03-1
ISBN: 1-933895-03-9
PCN: 2006935591

Managing Editor: Maggie Canon
Project Editor: Mireille Majoor
Cover and interior design: Diana Van Winkle

Bulk Discounts and Special Sales
Better Business Bureaus, corporate purchasing, colleges, consultants:
The Planning Shop offers special volume discounts as well as supplemental materials for BBBs universities, business schools, and corporate training. Contact:
info@PlanningShop.com
or call 650-289-9120

The Planning Shop™ is a division of Rhonda, Inc., a California corporation.

Cover photos © iStockphoto.com/Robyn Mackenzie, Sean Locke, Jeffrey Smith, Sawayasu Tsuji

"This publication is designed to provide accurate and authoritative information in regard to the subject matter covered. It is sold with the understanding that the publisher and author are not engaged in rendering legal, accounting, or other professional services. If legal advice or other expert assistance is required, seek the services of a competent professional."
— *from a Declaration of Principles, jointly adopted by a committee*
of the American Bar Association and a committee of publishers

Distributed by National Book Network

Printed in Canada

10 9 8 7 6 5 4 3 2

A Message from BBB President Steven Cole

B uying a home is the biggest financial commitment most consumers make. Having a trusted source to guide you through the home-buying process means you'll find a property that fits both your lifestyle and your financial goals. That source is the Better Business Bureau.

The *Better Business Bureau Buying a Home: Insider's Guide to Success* walks you through every step of purchasing a home—from finding one that's in good condition to picking an agent who'll look out for your best interests to understanding your rights and obligations when you sign the final contract. Knowing what to expect, what to ask, and what to look for will increase the chances of finding your dream home with few hassles.

When you buy a home, you'll come into contact with many different kinds of businesses—real estate agencies, inspection services, banks, title companies, and others. The BBB fosters fair and honest relationships between businesses and consumers, which means that during any step of this process you can check up on the companies and services you're doing business with. And the BBB provides extensive services for consumers, including free Reliability Reports, arbitration services, and best-practices standards to name just a few. For more information, see pages v-vii or check our website at *www.bbb.org*.

This book will help you navigate the often confusing waters of buying a home. We interviewed experts from more than 380,000 BBB members to find out what you need to know, which pitfalls to avoid, and the best resources to use when purchasing your home. The expertise and experience of BBB members provide insights you won't find in any other book.

Steven J. Cole
President and CEO
Council of Better Business Bureaus

According to a recent Gallup poll, 85 percent of Americans prefer to do business with a BBB member. In this book, you'll get the same reliability, dependability, and impartiality that consumers have come to expect from the BBB.

What Is the Better Business Bureau?

W hether you're checking out a new home builder's reputation or need help resolving a dispute with a local business or want to find out more about a charity you're checking out, the Better Business Bureau (BBB) supplies both consumers and businesses with the information they need.

With more than 150 independent local bureaus across the United States and Canada, BBBs contribute in a wide variety of ways to their communities. Local bureaus compile Reliability Reports, track and respond to complaints about businesses, arbitrate disputes, maintain websites where consumers can research companies and learn about local issues and scams, and work to encourage businesses to commit to delivering goods and services with integrity.

With consumers' help, the BBB is usually the first national group to learn of problems in specific industries. The BBB was on the front lines of the automobile "lemon law" debate in the 1980s. Individual states got on board, and with the BBB's assistance, enacted "lemon laws" to protect consumers who purchase defective motor vehicles.

Through the BBB's national website (*www.bbb.org*) and local bureaus, the BBB helps consumers determine whether companies and services are reputable. The BBB does this in many ways:

1) Consumer Complaints (see page x for how to file a complaint)

2) Reliability Reports (see page viii for how to access these reports)

3) Dispute Resolution

4) Code and Performance Standards

5) Online Certification Programs

6) Articles and Videos

Dispute Resolution

The BBB offers a binding arbitration program to people and/or businesses in need of resolving a marketplace dispute. The BBB provides a professionally trained arbitrator who listens to both sides, weighs the evidence, and makes a decision about the dispute. (While most bureaus provide this as a complimentary service, some charge non-member companies.)

Code of Advertising

Protecting consumers from deceptive and unfair advertising is at the heart of the BBB's mission. The BBB publishes a Code of Advertising that all members must adopt. The directives contain very specific rules, including when it is and is not appropriate to use terms such as "free," "factory direct," and "list price."

What the BBB Isn't

1) The BBB does not protect its own. The organization produces reports on, and conducts investigations into, both member and non-member companies.

2) The BBB is not a government agency. It is a private, non-profit organization funded by membership dues and other support.

Online Business Reliability Certifications

For companies selling products and services online, the BBB provides an online certification program. The **Online Reliability Seal** means that a company is a BBB member, has met the BBB's Code of Advertising, has been in business for at least one year, and is committed to dispute resolution to address customer complaints.

Articles and Videos

The BBB website (*www.bbb.org*) contains more than 800 free articles on topics ranging from "Work at Home Schemes" to "Choosing an Assisted Living Facility." For a complete list of articles, go to *www.bbb.org/alerts/tips.asp*.

The BBB also produces educational videos on various businesses, services, and products. The content is developed through extensive research, interviews with industry leaders, and reviews of consumer complaints. For a complete list of videos go to *www.bbbvideo.com*. The videos are available for purchase but can also be found at most libraries.

The BBB is supported by more than 400,000 local business members nationwide. It is dedicated to fostering fair and honest relationships between businesses and consumers, instilling consumer confidence, and contributing to an ethical business environment.

BBB Membership Requirements

To be a member of the Better Business Bureau, a company must:*

1) Be in business at least six months

2) Pay annual dues, determined by the size of the company

3) Meet all relevant licensing and bonding requirements

4) Respond promptly to all customer complaints and make a good faith effort to resolve all complaints

5) Cooperate with the BBB to eliminate any underlying causes of customer complaints

6) Comply with decisions rendered through the BBB's arbitration programs

7) Adhere to BBB standards in its advertising and selling practices

8) Agree to use the BBB name and/or logo only in the manners specifically authorized by the BBB

9) Support the principles and purposes of the BBB and not engage in any activities that reflect adversely on the Bureau

*These are nine of the 13 minimum membership requirements. To see all 13, go to *www.bbb.org/membership/standards.asp*. Some local bureaus may have additional requirements.

How to Check on a Company

hen determining which company or service to use as you hunt for a home, the BBB can help you investigate a company's past performance to find out whether any complaints have been lodged against them. This process is called a Reliability Report (*www.bbb.org/reports.asp*), and in 2006, the system offered Reports on 2.8 million U.S. and Canadian companies.

Reliability Reports list each company's name, address, phone number, fax, and contact person's name and email address. They also show if, and how, the company has resolved past disputes and if any actions have been taken against the company and/or its principals by government agencies. The BBB posts three years' worth of complaints for each company.

Complaints cover advertising issues, contract disputes, billing/collection issues, sales practices, customer service problems, repair problems, guarantee/warranty issues, product problems, refund/exchange issues, and a category labeled "undefined issues." For example, one company's Reliability Report had the following information: "This company has an unsatisfactory record due to its failure to respond to one or more complaints. The Bureau processed a total of 415 complaints about this company in the last three years; 191 in the past year."

You may search for information on a company that isn't yet in the BBB database. The Bureau generally waits until it receives three inquiries before starting a file on a particular company.

If you don't have access to a computer, you can receive a hard copy of a company's Reliability Report by calling your local BBB.

Information, Please

The BBB received 86 million requests for assistance and 41.5 million requests for Reliability Reports in 2005, a 52 percent increase over 2004. The largest number of requests concerned:

1)   Mortgage companies: 1.2 million

2)   Roofing contractors: 1.1 million

3)   Moving companies: 1 million

4)   Work-at-home advertisers: 963,820

5)   General contractors: 886,274

6)   New car dealers: 735,891

7)   Home builders: 610,548

8)   Construction & remodeling services: 547,926

9)   Auto repair & service shops: 495,113

10) Swimming pool contractors: 472,202

How to File a Complaint

W hen a company says something in its ads that isn't true or sells you a product that doesn't work and refuses to fix the problem, even after you've complained, what can you do? Some of us would stew about it, maybe tell a few friends, and refuse to ever do business with that company again. But you can take action (and help other consumers) by filing a formal complaint at *http://complaint.bbb.org*.

The BBB launches investigations, sometimes in conjunction with law enforcement agencies, whenever:

1) There is a pattern, or especially a large number of inquiries or complaints, about one particular company

2) A company's offer is unusual or suspicious, is large in dollar value, or affects a vulnerable group (senior citizens, for example)

3) A company's principals will not cooperate with or provide the BBB with requested information

Because of this complaint system, the BBB is often the first organization to know about potential scams and troubling trends in particular industries. When a scam develops in one part of the country, the news travels quickly between BBB offices in the U.S., Canada, and Puerto Rico, and these offices, in turn, alert the media and the public. The BBB handled more than 1.1 million consumer complaints in 2005 and conducted 3,100 investigations.

Once you've filed a complaint, the BBB will send a letter to the offending company to confirm that you truly are/were a customer and to get their side of the story. If you want additional information or need assistance with a complaint, please contact your local BBB, visit the BBB website (*www.bbb.org*), or call (703) 276-0100.

The top recipients of consumer complaints in 2005:*

1) Cellular phone service & equipment providers: 31,671

2) New car dealers: 23,572

3) Furniture stores: 14,553

4) Internet service providers: 14,523

5) General contractors: 12,693

6) Collection agencies: 11,897

7) Banks: 11,648

8) Telephone companies: 10,638

9) Credit card companies: 10,423

10) Auto repair & service shops: 10,371

* The BBB AUTO LINE program is counted separately. It handled 37,862 complaints involving automobile warranty claims in 2005.

About The Planning Shop

The Planning Shop, a nationally recognized publisher of quality books for entrepreneurs, is proud to publish the Better Business Bureau Insider's Guides to Success. The first three titles in the series are: *Buying a Home*, *Starting an eBay Business*, and *Buying a Franchise*.

The Planning Shop, located in Palo Alto, California, specializes in creating business resources for entrepreneurs. The Planning Shop's books and other products are based on years of real-world experience, and they share secrets and strategies from CEOs, investors, lenders, and seasoned business experts.

The Planning Shop's books have been adopted at more than five hundred business schools, colleges, and universities. Hundreds of thousands of entrepreneurs and students have used The Planning Shop's books to launch businesses and create business plans in every industry.

CEO Rhonda Abrams founded The Planning Shop in 1999. An experienced entrepreneur, Rhonda has started three successful companies. Her background gives her a real-life understanding of the challenges facing people who set up and run their own businesses. The author of numerous books on entrepreneurship, Rhonda's first book, The *Successful Business Plan: Secrets & Strategies,* has sold more than 600,000 copies and was acclaimed by *Forbes* and *Inc.* magazines as one of the top ten business books for entrepreneurs. Rhonda also writes the nation's most widely circulated column on entrepreneurship and small business.

Successful Business Strategies appears on USAToday.com and Inc.com and in more than one hundred newspapers each week. She is also the small business columnist for Yahoo Finance.

The Planning Shop's other lines of books include:

The **Successful Business series**, assisting entrepreneurs and business students in planning and growing businesses:

- *The Successful Business Plan: Secrets & Strategies*
- *Six-Week Start-Up*
- *What Business Should I Start?*
- *The Owner's Manual for Small Business*

The **In A Day series**, enabling entrepreneurs to tackle a critical business task and *Get it done right, get it done fast*™

- *Business Plan In A Day*
- *Winning Presentation In A Day*
- *Trade Show In A Day*
- *Finding an Angel Investor In A Day*

Books published by The Planning Shop are available in bookstores across the country and online at *www.PlanningShop.com*.

Table of Contents

SECTION 1: FIND YOUR DREAM HOME

SECTION 2: LOCATION, LOCATION, LOCATION

SECTION 3: CHOOSE THE RIGHT AGENT

SECTION 4: SECURE FINANCING

SECTION 5: INVESTIGATE THE MARKET

How Long Does It Take to Buy a Home?

"*It depends completely on the market. In a seller's market, my clients are lucky to find four or five houses that meet their criteria, and they need to jump on any property they like—usually within a week of viewing it for the first time. In a buyer's market, they might view as many as twenty to thirty homes, and take months to make an informed decision.*"

Pat Perelli, Realtor and BBB member,
John Hall & Associates,
Phoenix, Arizona

Find *Your* Dream House

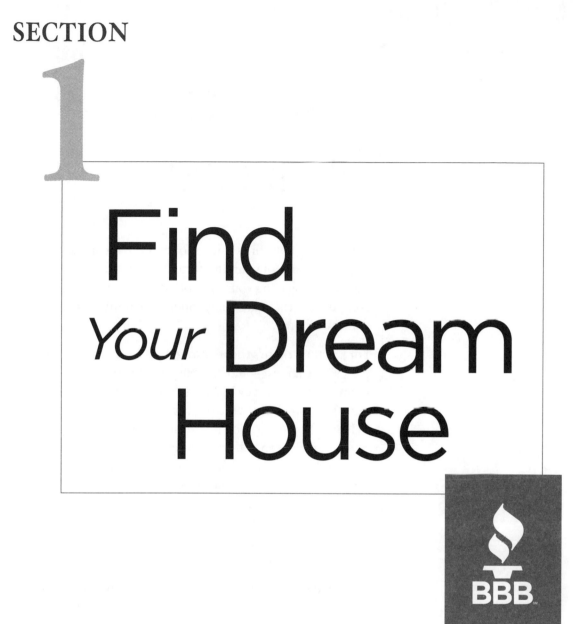

Take the Plunge

B uying your first home is one of the most exciting ventures of your life. It ranks up there with choosing a college or getting your first job. Besides the emotional component, there are many tangible benefits to owning your own home.

For starters, there's the investment. A house is most people's single largest—and typically most profitable—investment. A recent survey by Wells Fargo Home Mortgage revealed that almost nine of every ten renters in the U.S. believe a home is a good financial investment, and almost seven of every ten believe owning a home is very important to their long-term financial success. These positive attitudes don't change once a home is actually purchased. According to the same survey, 97 percent of first-time home buyers would never go back to renting, and 77 percent of first-time home buyers believe buying their home is the best investment they ever made.

And Uncle Sam *really* wants you to own your own home! As a homeowner, you get substantial tax advantages that can make a real difference to your financial well-being. For example, most, if not all, of the interest on your mortgage is deductible, as are your property taxes. So whether you're looking for a Victorian in San Francisco, a condo in New York, a brownstone in Chicago, or a rancher in San Antonio, chances are good that home ownership will contribute significantly to your overall lifetime earnings.

Then there's the fun stuff about home ownership. You can choose the paint, the carpet, and the window treatments. You can plant what you like in the garden. You can choose your own appliances and decide for yourself if you'd like a pet, a pool, or a basketball court. In short, you have choices—and control.

Whether you're single or married, starting a family, or investing with a partner or friend, you want to find the perfect home for you, one that fits your lifestyle, your budget, and your investment goals. And since investing in a home is a major financial step, the better you understand the process, the likelier it is you'll find the right home at the right price.

The definition of the "right" home is different for everyone. Some people want to move into a brand new home and not worry about fixing anything, while others are willing to buy an older home and fix it up. Still others would rather not do any yard work or maintenance, so a condominium is appealing. There are options for everyone's needs, and with a little research and legwork, you *can* find and buy the perfect home.

Types of properties

A "home" can be many things. It can be a single-family house with a yard and white picket fence in the midst of a family-oriented suburb. It can be a high-rise condominium in the middle of a major metropolis. Or it can be a rancher on six acres of land. The kind of dwelling you choose depends on the characteristics of the local market, your budget, your lifestyle, and your desire to be close to—or away from—neighbors.

The two basic kinds of residences:

Detached, single-family home. This is exactly what it sounds like. A freestanding building on a legally delineated parcel of land, a detached home doesn't share walls with any other dwelling and is designed to be lived in by one family.

Tax Breaks

For a quick estimate of how much you will save by buying a home, ask your agent to help you calculate the annual interest you will pay for your mortgage. Then add the property taxes (your agent will almost certainly be able to provide this information). This is how much you can deduct from your annual earnings. (Keep in mind that the total will depend on your tax bracket.) You'll quickly be able to see how much you'll save by buying instead of renting.

Stay in the Middle of the Road

Detached houses in the middle of a block are more sought after—and therefore more expensive—than corner lots. The noise and bustle of being so near an intersection lowers the desirability and the price of a house on the corner.

You will generally find single-family homes in areas where land is more plentiful and therefore less expensive. Depending on the area—and on zoning regulations—a detached home can sit on multiple acres of land or spread to the very borders of a small lot. No matter what type of single-family home you choose, you're opting for a lifestyle that provides you with a certain amount of privacy and control. Because your dwelling is freestanding, you don't have to worry about noisy (or nosy!) neighbors beside—or above or below—you. And because you own the property as well as the building, you can decide, within zoning limitations, what to do with your home and your land.

However, single-family homes are more expensive, which can put them out of the range of many first-time home buyers—and all maintenance, repairs, and improvements are your responsibility. Still, single-family homes appreciate more during good times and hold their value during downturns in the housing market. Many real estate experts suggest that first-time home buyers purchase detached homes whenever possible.

Attached dwelling. A number of residence types fall into this category, including town homes, condominiums, and co-ops.

- A town home is generally considered to be a full-sized (or nearly full-sized) house that is attached on one or both sides to other, similar townhouses.

- A condominium is one of multiple, privately owned units in a single building.

- In a co-op, you share ownership of an entire building with the other co-op owners.

In a condominium you get a deed for your particular unit, and you share ownership of the common areas and the exterior structures. In a co-op you get a "share" of the total building—in effect, you are a co-owner of the entire complex. You—and your neighbors—can make rules that limit whom you can sell your units to.

The advantages of any form of attached dwelling include lower cost (generally) and reduced individual maintenance. With the exception of some town homes, where you own a small patch of land and your own driveway, you don't have a yard or driveway to maintain. All duties and expenses involved in the repair and upkeep of the property as a whole are shared by all the owners in the complex. So you don't have to worry about maintaining the roof, shoveling snow, or cutting the lawn. The homeowners' association/co-op association takes care of this. Of course, you pay for those services in the form of monthly association or homeowner's dues, which can add substantially to the cost of ownership. These dues are not usually tax deductible.

The logistics of the actual day-to-day management of attached property varies. Sometimes the homeowners' association hires a third-party property management company to take care of general maintenance issues; sometimes a volunteer board handles these matters; and sometimes participation is required from individual owners.

Protect Your Privacy

One concern many people have about attached residences is lack of privacy. Your neighbors are close—too close in some cases. Their lives can intrude upon yours in the form of noises, smells, and eyesores. Disputes among owners are not uncommon, which is why the homeowners' association frequently also acts as a mediator. And there's the control issue. When you purchase an attached home, you agree to the Covenants, Conditions, and Restrictions (CC&Rs) of the association, which can include restrictions on everything from the types of window treatments you are allowed to use to which objects can be kept on balconies to rules on running businesses from your unit.

QUICK TIP

Do the Numbers

Don't assume a condo or co-op will be your cheapest option. To properly compare the monthly costs of owning a dwelling like this against the cost of a detached home, add the monthly fees associated with condo or co-op ownership to the cost of the mortgage and compare that number to the mortgage for an attached home. That way you can make sure you aren't paying more than you would for a single-family home of the same general size with the same features.

INSIDER'S INSIGHT

**Prequalifying
for a Mortgage**

"*The very first thing you do is
to go and get prequalified for
a loan. The lender will tell you
exactly how much you can
afford to spend, and you need
to know this upfront so that
you can be realistic about your
wants and needs.*"

Mike Dawson, Broker,
RealCo,
Fresno, California

The home-buying process: A snapshot

Knowing what to expect during the home-buying process will allow you to enjoy the adventure while managing the stress.

- **Prequalify for a loan.** Before you start considering anything else about home buying, it's important to understand approximately how much a lender will be willing to advance you in the form of a mortgage.

- **Figure out what you want versus what you need.** This will save you enormous amounts of time. Make a list of what you'd most like in your dream home—as well as the bare minimum you can accept.

- **Select a specific area.** The more specific you can be about where you want to live, the faster everything will fall into place.

- **Find a good agent.** Most people choose to work with a real estate professional when buying their first house. A good agent will do everything from helping you target your housing needs to isolating the properties that fulfill those needs to showing you the properties, helping you make an offer, navigating through the paperwork, and finally, closing the deal. Taking the time to find the right agent pays off later.

- **Look at properties.** At this stage you'll begin to see what you can expect in your selected area, given your requirements and price range. Although it can be sobering to bump up against the reality of the market, it's also exciting to match actual properties with your dreams.

- **Pick the right house.** The next step is to narrow down your choices by using the lists of priorities you've already established and doing comparative market analyses (CMAs) on a handful of properties (see page 35). Eventually, you'll be ready to take the plunge on the "one."

- **Negotiate the best deal and make the offer.** Here is where your agent's skills and experience really come in handy. Enlist their help when it's time to come up with the right price and terms for your offer. Depending on the market, your dream property may fall easily into your hands—or you may have to fight for it.

- **Arrange for inspections.** Termites? Foundation problems? Dry rot? You'll need to hire specialists to examine the house and report on any flaws.

- **Get financing.** You may already have been preapproved for a loan before you started the home-buying process, but now it's time to nail down your financing. How much should you put down? Do you want a 15- or 30-year mortgage? An adjustable or fixed interest rate? The help of seasoned professionals is invaluable here.

- **Open escrow.** Escrow is a legal arrangement in which an asset—usually a substantial sum of money but sometimes another kind of asset—is given to an independent third party to be held in trust until the conditions of a real estate contract have been fulfilled. (These are conditions that you and the seller of a property have agreed to, such as passing inspections.)

- **Close the deal.** You've never seen paperwork like the paperwork involved in a home purchase closing. Don't let the sheer volume of documents intimidate you. Your agent (or lawyer, depending on what part of the country you live in) will be by your side to help. At the end of it all, the keys are in your hands!

QUICK TIP

Reduce Your Stress

Chances are you're simultaneously thrilled and stressed at the thought of owning a home. Manage this stress by:

- **Talking to people.** Listen to stories about home buying—both good and bad—from friends, family, and co-workers, and ask them if they're glad, in the end, to be home owners.

- **Educating yourself about the local market.** Pick up real estate magazines, go to open houses, and read the ads in newspapers. Knowledge will go a long way toward reassuring you that you're up to the challenges, as well as the pleasures, of what lies ahead.

How Much House Can You Afford?

There's no point in lusting after that five-bedroom colonial on three acres of land if you only have the resources to purchase a two-bedroom starter home. A quick way to estimate which properties will be in the ballpark for your budget is to go to one of the many mortgage calculators on the Internet. Two free calculators that don't require you to register or provide any personal information are: *http://www.bankrate.com/brm/mortgage-calculator.asp* and *http://www.interest.com/content/calculators/monthly-payment.asp*.

They can give you a quick estimate of what your monthly payments would be based different home prices, mortgage terms, and interest rate scenarios.

Calculate your total monthly costs using this worksheet. You may have to do some research on local property taxes and insurance rates (your agent can help you with this) before you can fill in all the blanks. But it will be worth your time to gather this data before you actually begin looking at properties.

Monthly mortgage: _____

Property taxes (calculated on a monthly basis): _____

Homeowners' insurance (calculated on a monthly basis): _____

Utilities: _____

Maintenance/dues/assessments for condos, gated communities, or co-ops: _____

Total monthly cost of owning the property: _____

QUICK TIP

How Much Is Too Much?

Although *you* might feel comfortable with the monthly payments you calculate based on the worksheet above, your lender may not be. Once you have given the lender all the basic information they need, they will perform a quick calculation in order to prequalify you for a certain size loan—based on your *debt-to-income ratio*. To arrive at this ratio, your lender takes the percentage of your total income that you already owe to creditors and calculates how much you can safely borrow on top of that. Most lenders will not approve a mortgage in which the total percentage of your housing cost is larger than 28 percent of your income. (See page 52 for more.)

Separate "Wants" from "Needs"

T he first step in looking for a home is to distinguish between what you *must have* and what you would *like*. Do you absolutely need three bedrooms to accommodate your family but think four would be nice? Will two bathrooms suffice or are three a necessity? Do you want a large backyard or are you unable to deal with yard maintenance? How important is it to have an attached garage?

As you consider what you want, do some online research to help you put together a wish list for your dream home. Enter your region's name and "real estate" as keywords into any search engine. The sites that are returned will allow you to check out the general features and prices of properties in your desired area, view photos, and even take virtual video tours of specific houses or condos.

What matters to you?

Fill the worksheet on page 12 to narrow down what you need—and want—in a home. Take the worksheet with you when you start shopping for real estate agents and touring houses. It will help you articulate what you're looking for and remind you of the objective requirements of your home search at the moment when you're most likely to be charmed by properties that might not be appropriate.

INSIDER'S INSIGHT

Go Online

" *Because people are so Internet savvy, most realtors have websites. On my website, for example, I offer a lot of information that people can use to do their preliminary research on what properties are available and what the prices are, as well as giving them a step-by-step overview of what they can expect during the entire home-buying process.* "

Sam Silver, Realtor,
VIP Properties,
Valencia, California

What Matters to You?

FEATURE	MUST HAVE (NEEDS)	WOULD LIKE (WANTS)	N/A
Number of levels (stairs/no stairs)			
Number of bedrooms			
Number of bathrooms			
Yard			
Garage			
Parking available			
New home			
Older home			
Move-in condition			
Gas utilities			
Urban			
Suburban			
Rural			
Single-family home			
Condo			
Townhouse			
Pet friendly			
Mature landscaping			
Sunny			
Pool			
Separate office			
Close to transit			
Basement			
DSL/cable			
Near schools			
Near parks			
No neighbor noise			
No adjoining walls			
No one living above/below			
Low condo/maintenance fees			
Adults only			
Family friendly			
High-quality school district			
Brief commute time			
Gated community			
Disabled access			
Other			

The Child-Friendly Home

If you have (or are planning to have) children, certain features of the home and the neighborhood will be critical. A quality school district will be a major concern (see page 30 for more), but there are other considerations:

- **Low crime rate.** A safe neighborhood is at the top of the list. Check with the local police department, as well as local newspapers' police report logs. The Crime Lab at *www.homefair.com/homefair/calc/crime.html* offers the latest statistics on crime in particular cities. The National Sex Offender Database at *http://www.registeredoffenderslist.org* will help you investigate whether any convicted sex offenders live near a certain address.

- **Low-traffic street.** If you have young children, you'll prefer a street that is free from cars whizzing past at high speed. Check to see whether the road is a conduit to and from business districts, industrial parks, or other popular destinations.

- **Nearby playground.** Not having to load the kids into the car to get them outdoors is a time and stress saver, so look for a house within walking distance of a kid-friendly park.

- **Backyard.** A yard that's big enough for safe and fun play—and preferably enclosed by a fence or border foliage—is ideal for a growing family.

- **Appropriate floor plan.** You may want a single-level house to ease the burden (and noise) of having children thumping up and down stairs all day. Or you might opt for children's bedrooms that are close to the master bedroom.

- **Family room.** A separate room for kids to make messes as well as noise is something many families consider essential. Houses with "bonus rooms" or unfinished basements that can be easily converted into "rec" rooms are an option.

- **Neighbors with children.** Having other children on the block is great for kids and helps them integrate into a new situation.

INSIDER'S INSIGHT

Infuse Reality into Your Dreams

"It's a great idea to separate your wants from needs early on. But it's also important to be realistic. You don't want to get your hopes up only to have them dashed later. As a first-time buyer, you are very unsure of yourself, very sensitive. Be prepared to be flexible, even as you're defining your dream house."

Gary Love, Realtor,
Realty South,
Birmingham, Alabama

Separate "must have" from "won't tolerate"

When making choices about properties, what you don't want can be as important as what you do want. Hate noise? Then you won't want to live near an airport or train tracks. Have small children? Then a busy street is out of the question. Looking for peace and quiet? Then you don't want to be next to a playground. Just as certain features can make you eager to possess a property, others can cause you to veto it.

Identify the Dealbreakers

Complete the following worksheet to identify exactly what is and isn't acceptable to you. Show your real estate agent what you've come up with, and be sure to take the list along when you start looking at properties.

FEATURE	ACCEPTABLE	DEALBREAKER
Near train tracks or other noisy place		
Busy street		
Transitional neighborhood		
Fixer-upper		
Near commercial center		
Environmental risks (flood zone, electrical substation)		
Near school		
Visual pollution		
No garage		
No parking		
No basement		
No attic		
No yard		

FEATURE	ACCEPTABLE	DEALBREAKER
Close proximity to neighbors		
Shared walls		
No second (or third) storey		
Well water		
Other		
Other		
Other		
Other		
Other		

The Three L's

"*It's no accident that you'll hear the words 'location, location, location' from everyone you talk to about purchasing property. It really is the prime determinant of long-term value as well as a major contributing factor for how much you'll enjoy living in a particular home.*"

Lovinda Beal, Agent,
Cornish & Carey,
Portola Valley, California

Location, Location, Location

3

Your Perfect Neighborhood

Once you've identified what you need—and want— in a home, you must decide where you want that home to be. Perhaps you've heard that the three most important words in real estate are "location, location, location." This may be a cliché, but it is still extremely relevant. Even as you embark on the great adventure of home buying, you need to think about selling. Although the price you'll get for selling the house in the future will also depend on how well you maintain or improve it, the single biggest factor determining whether your investment will pay off is *where* your house (or condo, townhouse, or co-op) is located. "Location" is shorthand for a number of key attributes that make up a neighborhood, including the quality of the schools, access to mass transit or a major highway, proximity to services, quality of local construction, and the maturity of the landscaping.

Some buyers choose a house in an up-and-coming neighborhood, betting that its value will rise more quickly than if they purchased in an established area. Such a strategy can be risky. If the housing market takes a downturn, they could have trouble selling the property and recouping their

QUICK TIP

Through Traffic

Homes in residential neighborhoods that possess a higher percentage of cul-de-sacs and dead-end streets will carry higher price tags—and hold their value or appreciate faster—than houses in neighborhoods with through traffic.

initial investment. But buying in an up-and-coming location can also be a way for first-time home buyers to afford property in a geographic region that would otherwise be too expensive for them.

Special Events

When you're investigating a neighborhood, pay attention to whether it's in the vicinity of a stadium, concert hall, or college. Such landmarks signal that there will be sporting events, concerts, or festivals that will affect, at the very least, the traffic flow, and perhaps even the noise level, safety, and tranquility, of the surrounding streets.

What makes for the perfect neighborhood?

The "perfect" neighborhood is a matter of personal taste. Not everyone will have the same definition of what is ideal. Still, there are some features that most people will agree are particularly desirable when choosing a location:

- **Safety.** A low crime rate, absence of gang activity, and a vigilant police force are at the top of most home buyers' lists of neighborhood requirements.

- **Schools.** If you have children or are planning to start a family, the quality of the local schools is a top priority. School quality should also be a concern to those without children. That's because the quality of the school district is one of the prime drivers of real estate value. The resale value of your home—and how quickly you can sell it—often hinges on the rankings of the local schools.

- **Prestige.** Some addresses tend to confer a sense of higher social status on their residents than others. This might make a neighborhood more attractive to some people—and less attractive to others. Not surprisingly, houses in more prestigious neighborhoods carry higher price tags than those in less fashionable areas. Decide how important this "social premium" is to you—and how much extra you are willing to pay for it.

QUICK TIP

Go for the Worst

Take the time-honored advice to buy the worst house in the best neighborhood you can afford, rather than the best house in a less prestigious one. This kind of house tends to hold its value better in a slow real-estate market and appreciate faster in a hot one.

INSIDER'S INSIGHT

Look for the Jewel in the Rough

Say you find a beautiful new 3,500-square-foot house that you love, but it's in a neighborhood of older 2,000-square-foot houses, and costs a lot more than the rest of them. You have to be careful, because when it's time to sell, you might not get your money back. It's much better to find a house in a great neighborhood that has perhaps been neglected and needs remodeling. You may need to put $10,000 into it, but since the rest of the houses in the neighborhood sell for $40,000 or $50,000 more than that, it's well worth it.

Nancy Bristow, Realtor,
Emerald Coast Realty,
Pensacola, Florida

■ **Short commute time.** The distance between home and work—and the time it takes to travel between those places—is an important issue for many people. This is especially the case when gas prices are high. Consider the length of commute that you and your family can tolerate.

■ **Recreational facilities.** Do you like to exercise, participate in sports, or spend time outside? Then you'll want a neighborhood close to parks, jogging or biking trails, community baseball or soccer fields, or other recreational facilities.

■ **Shopping, restaurants, and movie theatres.** To many people, few things are more important than being within easy walking or driving distance of shops, restaurants, movie theatres, and other amenities. Having them readily available often tips the balance in favor of one neighborhood over another.

■ **Low traffic.** If you have, or are planning to have, children, or if you own a pet, chances are that living in a low-traffic area is high on your list. Traffic patterns are also a key consideration when taking future resale value into account. Properties on residential streets with no commercial traffic sell for more than comparable properties on busy roads.

■ **Lack of sensory pollution.** If a house is located downwind of a dairy farm, all the pleasure you take in the spacious porch, large yard, swimming pool, and mature landscaping could disappear when you encounter the odors and noise of such an operation.

■ **Parking.** If a property doesn't have a garage or assigned parking spot, or if you have too many vehicles to fit in the parking space provided (or a boat or an RV), the availability of on-street parking is critical. In many urban neighborhoods, it is difficult, if not impossible, to find parking during peak hours. And some communities limit, or even ban, on-street parking during certain times.

■ **Zoning.** Each community has its own, very specific, zoning laws that may regulate whether a particular property can be used for commercial purposes, restrict the kind and type of animals that can be kept there, specify what kinds of additions or improvements can be made, or even spell out the number and type of vehicles that can be parked on the premises. And a neighborhood that is zoned for both commercial and residential use—or one that is in transition from one purpose to another—can swiftly change character as properties are bought and sold. It's therefore critical to be aware of the zoning regulations of a particular neighborhood (see page 22 for more).

■ **Good ratio of owners to renters.** A neighborhood where most residents are owners will be more stable and experience less turnover than other kinds of neighborhoods. In general, upkeep of both buildings and lawns will be better in areas like this. And your chance of getting a mortgage, surprisingly enough, will also be greater, as banks consider the rent-to-own ratio as critical in gauging the value of a property.

■ **Weather.** In many parts of the United States, there are "microclimates"—geographic pockets in which the weather differs dramatically from other areas close by. Microclimates exist near bodies of water that cool the atmosphere and in urban areas where brick or asphalt absorb the sun and make the immediate vicinity hotter.

■ **Medical services.** If you need to be close to medical care, make sure the neighborhoods you are considering have the facilities that can meet your needs.

■ **Neighbors.** They will be a major factor in your enjoyment of your property. In some neighborhoods, residents mostly keep to themselves. In others, neighbors regularly hold block parties, community garage sales, and parades. Some communities are made up of retired residents; others are full of young families. Determining your needs in this regard is one of the most critical things you can do.

Go Green

The presence—or in some cases, absence—of trees, shrubs, and other mature foliage matters enormously in determining the character and desirability of a neighborhood. Many people like their property to have a vibrantly green look. Then there's the desire for shade—in hot climates, people use trees to keep a house cool and reduce the cost of utilities.

On the other hand, some people prefer a more minimalist look. And some owners of backyard pools like to clear away any vegetation that throws a shadow. Other people absolutely require the light and warmth of sun shining through their windows.

Whatever your ideal, make sure to consider it when putting together your list of desirable neighborhoods.

In the Zone

Owning a piece of property doesn't mean you can do whatever you like with it. Federal, state, and local governments use zoning laws to control how land is developed and what it is used for—including residential, industrial, agricultural, and commercial activities.

Just because one block is zoned residential doesn't mean there can't be commercial, or even industrial, activity going on in the next block. Specific attributes—and even the terms used to describe the various zoning classifications—vary dramatically from one location to another, even within the same county. It's important to understand precisely what zoning laws apply to the neighborhood you are interested in, as well as to adjoining ones.

You might want to convert a garage into a studio, build an in-law unit, or store an oversized RV on your property. And you may or may not be able to do these things based on the zoning. But don't think of zoning as something that exists to limit your options. Zoning laws also protect you. Your neighbors might not be able to build a view-blocking second story on their house. The owners of the house down the street may not be allowed to convert it into a beauty parlor. And it's quite possible that the empty lot down the street can't be used to raise chickens.

Zoning ordinances and maps are public records, so you can find out the zoning for a particular neighborhood by going to the local city hall or zoning office and asking for copies of the local ordinance (usually organized by zip code). Some communities have their zoning maps and ordinances online and even in libraries.

QUICK TIP

Attention All Control Freaks

Property values tend to rise faster in neighborhoods with strict zoning laws and well-organized neighborhood groups, mainly because these laws and groups ensure more stability, manage commercial development wisely, and keep the building of new homes to a minimum.

Your Ideal Neighborhood

Rank the following neighborhood features on a scale of 1 to 10, where 10 is "most desirable" and 1 is "not important." Keep your rankings in mind as you discuss potential neighborhoods with your real estate agent, family, and friends, and as you explore neighborhoods you are considering.

ATTRIBUTE	RANKING 1–10	NOTES
Good-quality schools		
Respected/prestigious address		
Safety		
Easy commute		
Medical facilities nearby		
Recreational facilities nearby		
Other amenities (shopping, restaurants, gyms)		
Childcare facilities nearby		
Low traffic		
Attractive surroundings (no "visual pollution")		
Low noise levels		
Odor free		
Easy on-street parking		
Residential zoning only		
High ratio of owners to renters		
Compatible neighbors/Strong sense of community		
Pleasant weather		
Other		

Choose the Right Neighborhood

ven before you choose an agent to help you begin looking at houses, there are some specific things you can do to narrow down the neighborhoods you wish to investigate. Here's where you need to perform your due diligence carefully. Use your own eyes and ears, and ask everyone who might have an informed opinion about various neighborhoods. That way, you'll be able to select an area that suits your particular needs.

- **Talk to residents**. This is the single most important thing you can do. Ask what they like/don't like about living in the neighborhood. Be specific in asking about schools, amenities, crime, and even neighborhood disputes.

- **Drive and walk around the neighborhood**. Do this at different times of the day, in the evening, and on different days of the week. The same neighborhood can look very different on a Monday morning than on a Sunday afternoon.

- **Research.** A local librarian should be able to point you to books, magazines, reports, websites, and other material that will give you data on a particular neighborhood. Visit the local police precinct to see crime reports. If there's a local paper, you'll be able to find articles about history, politics, social and economic developments, and current events. Don't forget to go to the city hall or local planning department to check on zoning issues or construction plans. The Internet is also an invaluable tool for helping to collect information about a particular area.

- **Attend a community meeting.** This will give you a handle on the larger issues facing the neighborhood, including zoning, legal issues, and crime.

- **Patronize the local merchants.** Browse through the stores and/or have a meal at a local restaurant. Ask the owners/managers what it's like to serve the residents of the area.

- **Hang out at the park.** If possible, go to the park at mid-day (or on the weekend) and interact with the parents and/or caregivers supervising their children at play. Such informal meetings often provide the most compelling insights into a community.

- **Do a practice rush-hour commute.** This is absolutely essential for determining whether or not a particular neighborhood will meet your needs.

Ask the neighbors

People who already live in a neighborhood are more knowledgeable about it than outsiders. In addition to using official resources, don't be shy about tapping into this source of intimate information. Strike up conversations at the laundromat, at the park, on the jogging trail, or at the community pool. Ask:

- Is there a sense of community? Are there any scheduled activities, such as block parties, group garage sales, parades, mothers' groups?

- Is this the type of neighborhood where you would feel safe walking around at night alone? Why or why not?

- How friendly are the local children toward new kids transferring into the district?

- Is any construction planned in the near future?

Rush Hour

Even the most peaceful neighborhood can turn into a parking lot during commute hours. Make sure your neighborhood isn't used as a shortcut to a major thoroughfare or industrial park during peak travel times. Visit the neighborhood(s) you are interested in during both the morning *and* evening commute hours. Traffic patterns can vary dramatically based on the primary direction of the commute to and from a local city or commercial hub.

- Has there been a lot of turnover in the neighborhood?

- What's the average age of residents? Are there mostly young families or mature individuals living here?

- Any bad blood in the neighborhood? Disputes between neighbors? Lawsuits?

- Any problems with crime? Drugs? Excessive noise?

QUICK TIP

Relocation Information

It's not uncommon for people to consider moving to a different city or state in order to be able to afford the house of their dreams. Previously, this kind of move required a great deal of time, money, and effort, as the information needed to make a wise relocation decision could be gathered only by traveling to the location itself, or in long-distance phone calls with local realtors or Chambers of Commerce.

That's all changed now. Through the Internet, it's easy to collect a broad array of data on remote locales. In fact, the main issue now is too much information! With so many realtors and Chambers of Commerce attempting to convince people to settle in their areas, it's easy to become overwhelmed by all the websites and online resources.

Although there are thousands of websites that let you look at properties for sale all around the world, here are a couple that can help you zero in on a particular city or neighborhood:

- *www.bestplaces.net* briefs you on everything from the demographics of the population—age, sex, ethnicity, education, religion—to the quality of the schools, average home prices, climate, cost of living, availability of mass transportation, and voting patterns. It even includes a "back fence" message board that allows users to leave candid messages about living in a particular locale.

- *www.homefair.com* provides comparisons of cost of living, climate, and demographics, as well as online calculators to help you estimate the true cost of relocating. A "relocation crime lab" feature gives you detailed information—by zip code—on crime statistics for a particular neighborhood.

Check out these resources before you make a move. You will be able to investigate—and eliminate—many neighborhoods, saving yourself time and money.

Rating Neighborhoods

Use this worksheet as you investigate different neighborhoods to rate what you see. Rank each feature on a scale of 1 to 10, with 10 being "highest quality" and 1 being "unacceptable quality."

If you're a numbers kind of person, you might want to sum up the various columns and see which neighborhood ranks highest on a purely numerical scale. Or you can use this worksheet to provide a quick snapshot of how the various neighborhoods rank against each other.

ATTRIBUTE	NEIGHBORHOOD 1	NEIGHBORHOOD 2	NEIGHBORHOOD 3
School quality			
Prestige			
Safety			
Commute			
Medical facilities			
Recreational facilities			
Other amenities (shopping, restaurants, gyms)			
Childcare facilities			
Traffic			
Surroundings			
Noise levels			
Smells			
Parking			
Zoning			
Ratio of owners to renters			
Neighbors/Sense of community			
Weather			
Other			

Who Are the People in Your Neighborhood?

Perhaps you want to live in the kind of neighborhood where you feel comfortable running over to your next-door neighbor's house to borrow a stepladder. Or one where the neighbors all have keys to each other's houses. Or you might like the privacy of a neighborhood where people largely mind their own business. Whatever your preference, there are a few things you can investigate about any neighborhood you are considering:

- **Demographics.** What's the average age of neighborhood residents? Education level? If you've already started working with a realtor, ask them. Chances are, particularly if they work regularly in particular area, they'll have insights for you. If you haven't yet chosen a realtor, a number of online resources, such as *http://realestate.yahoo.com/Neighborhoods* and *http://www.freedemographics.com* (requires free registration), can give you detailed demographic information by zip code.

- **Community involvement.** Some communities are sleepy and quiet; others are alive with activity.

Go to the library and ask to see back issues of the local newspaper (or go online and search through them electronically) to check out notices for garage sales, talent shows, or other organized events. Ask the local police precinct if permits have been issued for block parties or other events requiring street closings.

- **Neighborhood associations.** Is there a formal group that organizes and sponsors local events, works with the city to iron out local issues such as parking or zoning, and generally promotes a strong sense of community? To find out, ask a local business or go to *www.neighborhoodlink.com* and type in the area's zip code to see if a group like this is listed. Sometimes an informal group or motivated individual will take the lead in sponsoring potlucks, garage sales, and other neighborhood activities. Check out bulletin boards at local restaurants, coffee shops, and grocery stores to see whether these activities take place in your desired neighborhood.

New construction boom areas

New housing starts reached all-time highs in the early 2000s, with low interest rates motivating buyers to snap up new homes faster than builders could construct them. A new home has a lot of appeal just because everything is *new*. In addition to the "bones" of the house, condo, or townhouse—the foundation, plumbing, wiring, and structural underpinnings—there is the new flooring, built-in cupboards, and appliances.

But different considerations need to be taken into account when you're thinking about moving to a new *neighborhood*. The landscaping may be immature (or nonexistent), and ongoing construction can give the area an unfinished look. New schools don't have a sufficient track record for you to judge their quality. Local malls, grocery stores, or shopping districts might still be in the planning stages.

Because new development usually takes place farther away from the center of a city or other urban area, the commute into town can be longer. Frequently, the highway infrastructure that supports the influx of new residents to an area won't catch up to the creation of new subdivisions for years, leading to significant congestion and traffic delays.

Finally, there's the "ten-year-old-house" problem. Although in most communities, a house that is only a decade old would be considered quite modern, in places where there is a new housing boom and new houses are being erected continuously, a ten-year-old house can seem like a dinosaur—and that can make it very difficult to sell.

All the same, there can be real financial value in snapping up a new home in a still-developing neighborhood. Builders often offer incentives or special financing offers.

QUICK TIP

The Hidden Costs of Commuting

Although properties in outlying neighborhoods are usually less expensive than those closer to a city center, it's important to calculate the cost of the fuel you'll purchase and the highway tolls you'll pay for your commute. Consider the cost of additional childcare, as well. A long commute can add extra hours to your work day and to your childcare bill. This might make the monthly price of living in a relatively central neighborhood more attractive than you imagined.

The Good, the Bad, and the Noisy

If you have a child, you might think there would be nothing better than to live across the street or around the block from the school they attend. There's the short trip to and from classes every day, not to mention the possibility that your child may eventually be able to make the trip alone. Then there's the fact that you'll be close to after-school activities, playgrounds, and other recreational facilities.

But there are other factors to take into consideration. You might not like the noise—just drop by an elementary schoolyard during recess time and you'll find the volume can be intense. Then there's the congestion. During peak drop-off and pick-up hours—not to mention days when there are special sports events, performances, parades, and holiday celebrations—streets can be blocked, and the lack of parking can force residents to walk long distances just to get to their front doors.

All about schools

Few things contribute more to a neighborhood's desirability than the quality of its schools. Areas containing the highest-valued properties are almost invariably those with the most highly ranked schools.

There are a number of ways to check out school quality. First, find out which schools serve the neighborhoods you are interested in. Don't make assumptions or depend on hearsay. Go directly to the school board and ask to see a map. (Many cities have already put these online or allow you to enter a particular street address to verify what school a resident of that address would attend.)

The rankings of schools are usually available at the local library or online through the school's or school district's website. A useful online resource is *www.schoolmatters.com*, maintained by the research firm Standard & Poor's. You can enter the zip code, city, or school name and receive the latest test scores, rankings, ratio of students to teachers, and more.

Many principals will meet one-on-one with parents to discuss the school's agenda, mission, and strengths. Ask for a tour of the premises and for the opportunity to visit a classroom in session to judge the general climate and atmosphere of the facility.

Check out the Parent Teacher Association (PTA) or any other parent-run organization that contributes to a school's operations, curriculum, or agenda. Get the minutes of recent school board meetings, and attend one if possible.

School Research

Use this worksheet to record data during your interviews with school principals, administrators, parents, and neighbors. Make a copy for each school district you research. The answers to your questions about the quality of a certain school may make the difference between choosing one neighborhood over another.

QUESTIONS TO ASK	ANSWER	NOTES
Age of school		
Grades served		
Number of students attending		
Average class size		
Sports activities		
Art curriculum		
Music curriculum		
Honors classes		
Student clubs or other extracurricular activities		
Average tenure of teachers		
Average age of teachers		
Ranking of school in state		
Test scores		
Percentage of students going on to college		
Awards won		
Social dynamics		
Presence of gangs or cliques		
Problems with bullying, harassment		
Other		

How to Be Your Agent's Favorite Client

> *My favorite clients are the ones that know what they want. They've thought about it, researched it, and are realistic about it.*

Pat Perelli, Agent and BBB member,
John Hall & Associates,
Phoenix, Arizona

Choose *the* Right Agent

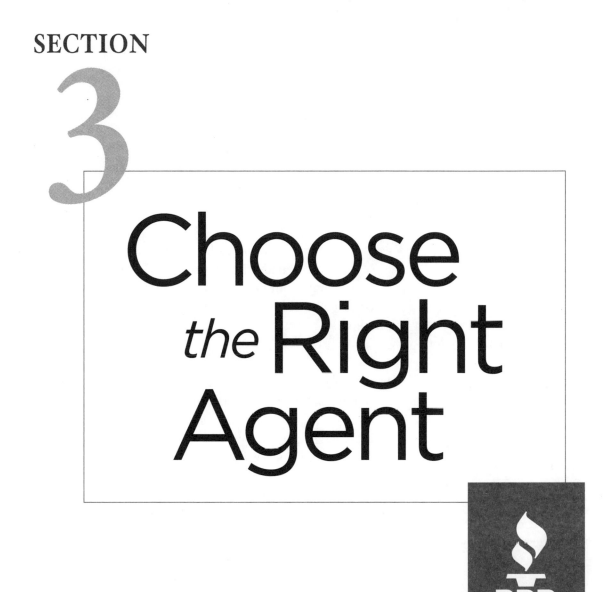

What Is an Agent?

B y defining your dream house and selecting your desired neighborhood, you've laid the groundwork for a very important decision: selecting the professional who will guide you through the rest of the home-buying process.

There are two broad categories of real estate professionals:

- **Agent (or salesperson).** To become a real estate agent in most states, a candidate must complete required coursework and then pass a state exam that tests their knowledge of a broad variety of real estate–related topics, including local zoning regulations, state disclosure laws, and ethical guidelines. In order to work legally, these salespeople must usually be associated with (and act under the authority of) a real estate broker (see below).

- **Broker.** After accruing experience in real estate sales, a salesperson may decide to become a real estate broker. Usually more coursework is required, and a broker's state exam must be passed. After obtaining a broker's license, a real estate agent may continue to work for another broker as a salesperson (often referred to as a broker associate), become a real estate office branch manager, or take charge of their own brokerage and hire other salespeople.

INSIDER'S INSIGHT

Everything Is Negotiable

Just because there are traditional ways of doing things—especially calculating agents' fees—doesn't mean they are written in stone. You can—and should—negotiate the cost of any service in the home-buying chain.

Lovinda Beal,
Agent, Cornish & Carey,
Portola Valley, California

Realtors can be either agents or brokers, although the word *realtor* is often used as a general term for anyone in the real estate industry. However, legally, the word *Realtor* is a registered trademark of the National Association of Realtors and shouldn't be used unless the agent in question is an NAR member. All Realtors are brokers and/or agents, but not all brokers/agents are Realtors.

In this book, all real estate professionals are referred to as *agents*.

The duties of a real estate professional

An agent is in the business of facilitating real estate transactions. If you have property to sell, they find you a buyer; if you are seeking property, they find someone who wants to sell. Agents provide a number of other specific services:

- **Showing properties.** An agent has relationships with other agents and brokers and has legal permission to show properties listed by other real estate professionals. Without an agent of your own, you would have to contact the seller's agent for each piece of real estate you wished to view.

- **Providing a comparative market analysis (CMA).** A CMA compares, feature for feature, one property against similar properties in the same neighborhood that have recently sold. Your agent prepares a CMA for every home you are interested in so that you can judge its value relative to others on the market.

Service à la Carte

A growing percentage of real estate professionals will offer "à la carte" services whereby they perform only one or a number of their customary functions for a negotiated fee. This is an option if you want to save money and feel comfortable doing a great deal of the research yourself.

For sellers, the advantages of à la carte real estate services are obvious: the fee they pay will be reduced if they are willing to do some of the work themselves. For buyers, the advantage is indirect: because sellers pay both the buyer's and the seller's agent's commissions, the seller benefits directly if the buyer uses à la carte services. But precisely because the overall fees are reduced, the buyer can frequently negotiate a better price on the home.

QUICK TIP

Buying under the Influence

Be wary of agents who are overly opinionated and who try to push you to buy a particular house, choose a particular lender, or otherwise unduly influence you. These things are *your* decision, and any agent who tries to bully you into making a choice you are not comfortable with should be dispensed with immediately.

Dual Agents

Occasionally, a single agent will act on behalf of both buyer and seller. When that happens, the agent is called a "dual agent." Sometimes you'll share an agent with a seller because both of you like and trust that person and believe they will act fairly. At other times, the motivation will be financial: if you see a property you like and don't yet have an agent, you might choose to use the seller's agent because the agent agrees to reduce the seller's commission and convinces the owner to discount the property proportionally. (The seller's agent could be motivated to do this because they are already receiving commission as both seller's and buyer's agent.) But consider all the factors carefully before you choose a dual agent—the potential for conflict of interest is significant.

- **Facilitating the offer.** Once you have found a property you like, your agent will work with you to come up with an offer and will identify any conditions—such as having the house pass inspections—that must be met before you close the deal.

- **Drawing up the contract.** Unless there is something highly unusual about the transaction, a standard contract will be used to draw up the agreement between you and the seller. Your agent will fill out the paperwork and make sure that the contract accurately reflects the terms of the offer.

- **Managing the logistics of fulfilling the contract.** An agent facilitates the escrow process (see page 144-143), helps you find a title company, coordinates with appraisers, inspectors, and contractors; processes the paperwork; and helps you manage all the logistical aspects of satisfying the terms of the contract.

- **Coordinates the closing.** If any last-minute complications arise, your agent helps you deal with them.

QUICK TIP

Why Use an Agent?

Although 85 percent of first-time home buyers use an agent, you don't have to. An increasing number of people are using the Internet to find and purchase property on their own. Keep in mind, though, that technically, the fee for your agent doesn't come out of your pocket—the seller pays. So going solo doesn't necessarily save you any money unless you are purchasing a for sale by owner (FSBO) property.

Who pays the agent?

Except under special circumstances (see page 36), your agent represents you and no other party involved in the transaction. The seller will also have their own agent, unless they are attempting a for sale by owner (FSOB) transaction (see page 44). But the relationships—and allegiances—are not as clear cut as you might expect, because of the way fees are calculated and paid.

In most states, the seller pays all the agents' fees, which can range from 3 to 6 percent of the selling price of the house. This puts your agent in a peculiar position, as the seller, not you, is paying the commission. Moreover, the higher the sale price, the more money your agent will make.

How can the your agent's compensation be reconciled with your goal of paying the lowest price for a property? Can you really depend on your agent to act solely on your behalf when they are, in fact, being paid by the seller?

This is one of the reasons that some buyers, despite all the potential benefits of having an agent, choose to go it alone. They simply don't feel comfortable depending on someone whose monetary interest may reside elsewhere. The agent's payment arrangement also makes it vital to choose an agent you like and trust. Throughout the home-buying process, trust in your advisor is critical.

What Agents *Don't* Do

If you're a typical first-time home buyer, you'll likely opt to go with an agent, rather than flying solo. But it's still important to have realistic expectations of what an agent will or will not do for you.

- **Devote all their time to you.** Your agent will have other clients. They aren't always on the spot precisely when you need them. It's important to have realistic expectations of the kind of attention you can expect from a busy agent.

- **Give you legal advice.** Even if you don't live in a state like New York, where the deal is primarily accomplished by a lawyer, your agent cannot provide legal advice. If there is anything about a deal that is legally complicated, hire outside counsel to be sure that you don't take a legal misstep.

- **Perform basic research on schools, zoning, and other technical issues.** Although good agents should have a strong working knowledge of the areas they serve, you can't depend on them to be the last word on critical aspects of a locale, including the school district or zoning issues. Using an agent doesn't get you off the hook for performing your own due diligence.

6

Go for
the Best

If, after knowing what agents can—and cannot—do for you, you decide to work with one, you will still need to consider a number of other things. Is a particular agent a good personal as well as professional fit? Is that mysterious "X" factor—chemistry—right between you?

A good agent:

- **Educates you about the home-buying process.** A good agent takes the time to answer all your questions and instructs you about the ins and outs of the particular market you face.

- **Has a compatible personality.** Choose an agent you feel comfortable with. You'll be providing this person with intimate details about your finances and lifestyle. And depending on the type of market, how particular you are about the property you purchase, or the terms of the contract, you may be spending quite a lot of time with your agent. Make sure it's someone you like.

QUICK TIP

Knowledge Is Power

A diligent agent won't wait until a client asks to see a particular piece of real estate; they will have visited that property as soon as it came on the market—either during an agents' tour or on their own. An agent who specializes in a particular neighborhood can sometimes even alert you to the possibility of purchasing a property before it is officially put up for sale.

QUICK TIP

Get Some Respect

Your agent's standing in the community can be a huge factor in determining whether or not you get your dream house. All other things being equal, when choosing between offers, a seller often goes with the client of the agent who is most respected. The primary reason is relationships: If agents have worked compatibly together in the past and are comfortable with each other's way of working, they will naturally gravitate toward doing deals together. Competence is another factor: an agent with a reputation for meeting deadlines and getting paperwork completed satisfactorily will always be more attractive than an agent who has sloppy work habits or is unreliable about the logistics of the process.

- **Takes the time to find out your needs and wants.** You should be able to tell from the very first meeting whether an agent is listening or not. Are they focused on you as you explain what you want? When they show you properties (either virtually, as in an online tour, or in a real visit), do they fall into the range of what you want? Of what you can pay for? Does the agent follow up on any questions you have that they can't answer immediately? If not, move on.

- **Can brief you on the ins and outs of particular neighborhoods.** Although it's helpful for an agent to have any general knowledge about the geographic area you are interested in, your needs will be better met if they have specific knowledge of the neighborhood(s) you are focusing on. A good agent should be able to tell you the basic demographics (who lives there, the average age, the average length of time people stay in their properties), as well as displaying more intimate knowledge of the area, such as the general friendliness and social involvement of the community.

- **Finds you the home that best suits your needs.** A good agent won't pressure you to make an offer on a home you don't like or a property that's outside your budget.

The Ethics Door

The ethics door swings both ways. Agents have ethical standards to meet, and you also have ethical responsibilities. For starters, if you are working with more than one agent, you should make that clear to all the agents you're dealing with. Since an agent gets paid only upon results—that is, when you actually buy a piece of property—asking them to spend time showing you around or answering your questions only to use a different agent to do the actual purchase is an ethical no-no.

Likewise, if you are just testing the market with no intention of buying for a significant length of time—say, not for 12 months or more—you should be upfront about that fact so the agent can make an informed decision about whether to invest time and effort in the relationship.

INSIDER'S INSIGHT

The Value of Loyalty

To me, a good client is a loyal client. If I'm working with a buyer, I'm going to give it my all, and I hope my clients will appreciate it and not go around to 10 different Realtors and every weekend go out with a different one.

Sam Silver, Realtor,
VIP Properties,
Valencia, California

■ **Tells you the truth.** Whether it's advising you against that dirt-cheap fixer-upper, or encouraging you to raise your offer on a particular property, a good agent will give you honest information.

■ **Processes the paperwork correctly, efficiently, and on time.** A good agent is well organized, keeps careful records, and meets deadlines.

■ **Directs you to reputable mortgage brokers, house appraisers, title officers, and local contractors.** The address book of a competent real estate agent should be jam-packed with contacts from banking, appraising, contracting, and legal services.

Find and Evaluate an Agent

I t's worthwhile to invest time in finding the right agent. After all, while you're searching for and negotiating for your perfect home, you'll be spending a significant number of hours with them—perhaps even more than with your spouse, partner, or best friend!

A number of avenues can be taken to find a good real estate professional:

- **Network.** Recommendations from friends, neighbors, colleagues, and family members are the best place to start. Collect names from everyone you know.

- **Go to open houses.** Open houses are rarely about selling homes—at least, not directly. Their main purpose, from the agent's point of view, is to attract more clients. For you, attending an open house is a good way to size up a particular agent. Visit as many open houses as you can, even if you're not interested in the property, and collect business cards.

- **Read the local paper.** Many agents take out ads promoting the properties they've listed. Check to see which ones are selling houses in your chosen neighborhoods.

- **Drive around your target neighborhood.** Looking at "for sale" signs is one of the chief ways that would-be homeowners find their agents. Contact the agents who have posted the most signs in your chosen area.

On a Handshake

Once you've found an agent you like and trust, you should tell them definitively that you've chosen to work with them. Stop using the services of other agents at this point and work exclusively with the one you've chosen. Note that you will have a verbal, not a written, agreement with your real estate professional. In fact, you should run, not walk, away from any agent who tries to get you to sign a contract saying you'll work with them exclusively for a specified amount of time.

When to Interview an Agent

Because agents are busiest during the weekends, schedule your interviews with them during the week. If you have a nine-to-five job, try getting away during your lunch hour or immediately after work. Most agents bend over backwards to accommodate clients and will work late into the evening if necessary.

Try to do the interview in the agent's office, so you can see how they run their business. Is their desk organized? Do they seem to be on top of their paperwork? Do they have an assistant to answer the phone or are they overextended by trying to run the office themselves? All these things will give you clues about the type of person you may be working with.

The activity list

One of the most important things you can do when interviewing potential agents is ask to see their "activity list." This is a detailed record of every property that person has sold in the previous 12 to 24 months. You might wonder why this would be important, given that you're seeking help in *buying* property. But an activity list can tell you a great deal about a particular agent's areas of interest and expertise, as well as their:

- **Success rate.** The more properties listed and sold, the more skilled the agent is at pricing and staging properties and helping clients close deals. A high success rate demonstrates business and negotiating acumen, ties to the community, and awareness of the true market value of property—all important things to *buyers* as well as sellers.

- **Knowledge of particular neighborhoods.** By seeing exactly where the houses an agent has sold are located, you have solid proof of this agent's experience with a particular neighborhood.

- **Familiarity with different types of properties.** Are you looking for a condo? A town home? Single-family home? Make sure the agent's activity sheet demonstrates experience with that type of property.

- **Experience with a specific *class* of properties.** If you're searching for a starter home, it's not a good idea to engage a real estate agent who specializes in high-end luxury homes.

- **Reputation.** Make sure that the activity list the agent gives you includes the names and contact information of previous clients, so you can get references.

Do You Need a Lawyer?

First-time home buyers frequently ask whether they need a lawyer. After all, the contract you sign with the seller is a legally binding document, and your real estate agent is not qualified to give you legal advice. In fact, you should probably question the competence and/or ethics of any agent who tries to do so.

In some states, lawyers have traditionally performed many of the duties involved in buying or selling real estate. This is the case in New York, for instance. In other states, it is extremely rare for a lawyer to get involved.

Several things determine whether you should use a lawyer. The first is the complexity of the transaction. If the purchase can be achieved with your agent's standard contract, you don't likely need formal legal advice. But in any special circumstances—for example, if there's a question about whose name is put on title—you should probably hire a lawyer.

Then there's what agents call the "sleep-at-night factor." If you're the nervous type, you might want to spend the money to have an experienced real estate lawyer look over the contract or preside over escrow or closing.

Time to say goodbye

Occasionally, buyers have problems with an agent. In many cases, they can work out whatever issues have arisen. But sometimes it's best to find another real estate professional. Say goodbye to any agent who:

- **Fails to listen to your wants and needs.** If you find communication difficult or if your agent doesn't seem to "get" what you're saying, try to improve your communication. Be clear about your concerns. If that doesn't work, you might have to walk.

- **Pressures you to act before you're ready.** Your agent is meant to be a supportive guide. So the last thing you want is to have them push you in a direction you don't like. Communicate your discomfort. If you still feel pressure, it's time to terminate the relationship.

- **Acts unethically.** If you have *reasonable* grounds to suspect that your agent is disclosing inappropriate information to the seller or the seller's agent or is otherwise not completely committed to your best interests, run, don't walk, away.

- **Misses appointments and deadlines or otherwise acts irresponsibly.** An agent who is habitually late or absent from important meetings, misses deadlines, messes up paperwork, or otherwise prevents the sale from proceeding is not one you should be working with.

- **Is incompetent.** Although your agent had to pass a test, this doesn't always guarantee that they will be skilled enough to complete a deal. Occasionally, an agent needs to be dismissed for incompetence.

- **Is a poor fit.** Sometimes the chemistry just isn't right. In that case, it's best for all parties to admit it and move on.

For Sale by Owner

A for sale by owner (FSBO) property is exactly what it sounds like: an owner has decided not to use an agent and is offering a property for sale directly to buyers. By eliminating an agent or broker from the transaction, the seller won't be obliged to pay the 3 to 6 percent commission that would normally be associated with the sale. According to the National Association of Realtors, 13 percent of U.S. real estate transactions in 2005 took place via FSBO.

Because the fees for a real estate transaction are traditionally paid by the seller, when a house is on the market on an FSBO basis, potential buyers may have difficulty engaging a real estate agent on their behalf. The only remedy would be to pay out of pocket for the agent's services.

If you like an FSBO property, do you have to give up on using an agent—or sacrifice your dream house? Not at all. Because the seller is saving money by not paying agent's fees, you might be able to convince them to give you a price break on the property and use that saving to pay your agent's commission. Because you likely found the FSBO house yourself (and therefore saved your agent time and effort), the agent might be willing to give you a discount on their typical fee.

Agent Evaluation

When you find an agent, call and ask for an in-person interview. Make a copy of this worksheet for each agent you interview, so you'll have a clear snapshot of each one. If all other factors are equal, always choose the one you feel most comfortable with—personality is the most important factor in determining whether your partnership will succeed.

Do you like this agent? Do you feel comfortable with this person?

_____

Do they seem to have a good understanding of the neighborhood?

_____

Can they answer your questions about the relative pricing of various properties in the targeted neighborhood?

_____

Can they provide you with references to call?

_____

Are they competent to discuss financing options?

_____

Did they take time to ask you questions about your wants and needs?

_____

Did they appear to listen and absorb what you had to say?

_____

Do they have experience with the type and class of property you're looking for?

_____

Do they have a wide network of industry contacts?

_____

Other concerns

_____

No Money Down?

"If you have an excellent credit score, you may be eligible for a program that allows you to get 100 percent financing, so all you have to pay to get into a property are the closing costs."

Nancy Bristow, Realtor,
Emerald Coast Realty,
Pensacola, Florida

Secure Financing

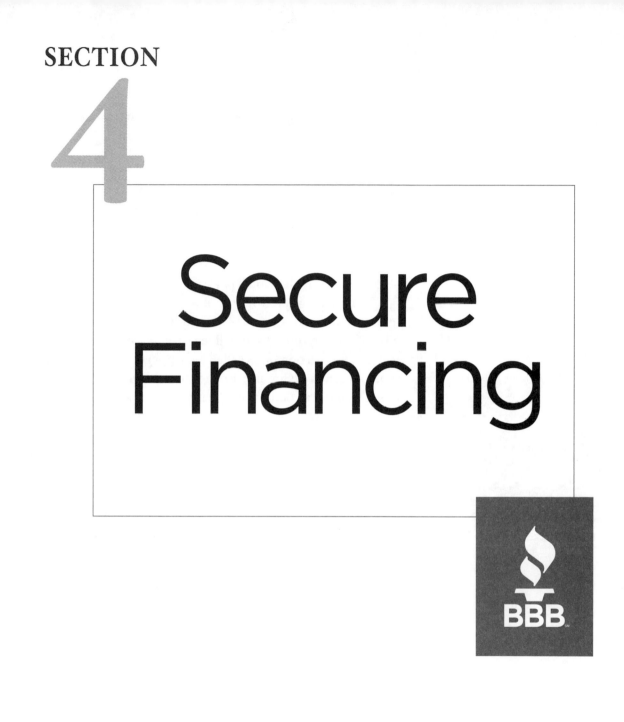

8

Something Borrowed

I t's unlikely that you'll pay cash for your first home. The average price a first-time buyer pays for a home in the United States is $150,000 —and few people have that kind of ready money. Most will have to borrow all or part of it. The sum you borrow is called a mortgage, which is a legal term of French origin first used in the 13th and 14th centuries. The modern definition of a mortgage is a loan secured by real estate or another valuable asset. (That is, if the loan is not repaid, the lender is in a position where they may seize that asset to make up for their loss.) Today, mortgages are the standard method of enabling individuals or businesses to purchase property.

Since a mortgage is a loan, it needs to be repaid. A mortgage is usually repaid in monthly installments, which are made up of two components:

- **Principal.** Part of each monthly payment reduces the size of your loan. If your mortgage is $200,000 when you start out, the total decreases with each monthly payment, until at the end of the term of the mortgage— often 30 years later— the balance is zero.

- **Interest.** You can't use a lender's money for free. The cost of a loan is called interest, and it is a percentage of the total amount borrowed. Part of each of your monthly mortgage payments is applied to the fee you are being charged for the privilege of using someone else's money.

Mortgage Brokers

Although you may work directly with a bank or other financial institution to arrange for a mortgage, you may also choose to work with a mortgage broker, who will act as an intermediary between you and multiple lenders in order to find the best loan to meet your needs.

The size of your monthly mortgage payment depends on a number of factors, including the size of your loan, the prevailing market interest rate, the type of loan you choose, and your credit history. Your mortgage is probably the single biggest expense you will ever incur. Understand all the options you have in selecting a loan and choose a lender carefully.

The mortgage application process

You apply for a mortgage using a formal process that is fairly standard no matter where you are located or what lender you choose. First, you fill out a mortgage application and provide documentation about your financial history to the institution that will be advancing the money.

One term you hear when applying for a mortgage is *under-writing*. Underwriting refers to the process that the bank or other financial institution uses to judge whether you are capable of repaying the debt. This generally involves reviewing your credit history from credit reporting agencies and checking on the state of your finances. A bank or mortgage broker will require any or all of the following information to accomplish this: salary payment stubs from your employer, income tax returns, bank statements, credit card balances, car loan documents, stock certificates, and documentation of any other assets or debts you possess.

Interest rates

An interest rate is the price you pay for the use of the money you are borrowing. It is one of the primary determinants of what you can afford. The lower the interest rate, the lower your monthly mortgage payments will be. Or, to put it in another way, the lower the interest rate, the bigger the loan you can afford. This is why the housing market booms when interest rates are low and turns sluggish as interest rates rise.

Internet Mortgages

An increasingly large percentage of first-time home buyers bypass traditional sources of mortgages and use the Internet to research, apply for, and secure financing. Some of the more popular sites walk you through a simple application process and then have a live representative call to discuss your options. Investigate a Web-based mortgage brokerage as you would any lender before entrusting it with your personal financial information.

Doing the Math

Interest rates can make a huge difference in what you'll be able to afford. If you're like most first-time home buyers, you probably have a rough idea of how much you can spend per month on your housing costs (more precise ways to estimate this will be presented later in this section). For example, you might currently pay $1,000 a month for rent and have determined that you can go up to $1,500 a month to purchase your home. The two charts below compare the total amounts your budget might allow you to borrow, based on various interest rates.

You'll see figures for both 15- and 30-year mortgages. The *length* of the loan is one of the major factors to consider when you are choosing a mortgage. The longer you take to pay back a loan, the lower your monthly payments will be. On the other hand, you'll pay more *interest* over the life of the loan if the duration of the mortgage is longer.

Given this, it's not surprising that you'd be able to afford much more home if you're able to get a 30-year mortgage at a 6 percent interest rate than if you agreed to a 15-year mortgage at a 10 percent interest rate. In the case of the 30-year mortgage, you'd be able to borrow more than $100,000 more! It's no wonder that people scramble to get into the housing market when interest rates are dropping.

It is very uncommon today for first-time home buyers to choose a 15-year mortgage, primarily because they are usually struggling to keep their monthly payments as low as possible.

INTEREST RATE ON A 30-YEAR MORTGAGE	APPROXIMATE MORTGAGE *PRINCIPAL* THAT CAN BE BORROWED FOR $1,500 PER MONTH (NOT INCLUDING DOWN PAYMENT). THE ACTUAL PRICE OF THE HOUSE YOU CAN AFFORD WILL BE HIGHER OR LOWER, DEPENDING ON HOW MUCH CASH YOU HAVE TO PUT DOWN.
6%	$250,000
7%	220,000
8%	195,000
9%	175,000
10%	160,000

INTEREST RATE ON A 15-YEAR MORTGAGE	APPROXIMATE MORTGAGE *PRINCIPAL* THAT CAN BE BORROWED FOR $1,500 PER MONTH (NOT INCLUDING DOWN PAYMENT). THE ACTUAL PRICE OF THE HOUSE YOU CAN AFFORD WILL BE HIGHER OR LOWER, DEPENDING ON HOW MUCH CASH YOU HAVE TO PUT DOWN.
6%	$180,000
7%	170,000
8%	165,000
9%	155,000
10%	145,000

Prequalifying for a loan

Prequalification means that a bank has tentatively agreed to give you a certain size of mortgage. Unlike an actual loan, however, which is calculated based on formal documentation, including your credit report, pay stubs, income tax returns, and credit card statements, prequalification is based, largely in good faith, on information provided by you, the prospective home buyer. You provide the name of your employer, state your monthly income, list all other assets, and estimate the amount of your current monthly debt. Some lenders will want to see a pay stub or other evidence of income, and most will want to run a credit report. But in general, you are being asked to provide an honest assessment of your own worthiness to take out a mortgage.

The best time to prequalify for a loan is the moment you decide to begin looking for a home to buy. You should do this even before searching for an agent (in fact, most agents won't take you seriously unless you have already been prequalified). There are typically time limits on a prequalification approval, after which you may need to reapply.

Keep in mind that any sum you prequalify for will be available to you only if you can jump all the hurdles of the *actual* loan application process after you've found the property you want to buy. No matter how badly you want to qualify for a certain size of loan, it is essential to be honest. Prequalifying may help you find an agent and may even allow you to win a bid on a house. (Most owners, especially in hot markets, won't consider offers from people who are not prequalified.) However, when it comes down to actually applying for the mortgage, the bank *will* be checking—and if you fudged any numbers, it will become obvious.

Honesty Is the Only Policy

When it comes to filling out your mortgage application, be ruthlessly honest. Not only is it futile to misrepresent yourself—after all, the lender will require extensive documentation that backs up your claims of income, existing debt, and so on—but you can get yourself into deep financial trouble by trying to borrow more money than a lender has determined is safe for you to take on. Legitimate lenders may reject your application if there's any evidence of a deliberate intention to deceive.

Debt-to-income ratio

Once you've given the lender all the basic information they need, they will perform a quick calculation in order to prequalify you for a certain size of loan. This is calculated through your *debt-to-income ratio*. This ratio takes the percentage of your total income that you already owe to creditors and calculates how much you can safely borrow on top of that. There are two industry-standard debt-to-ratio numbers: 28 and 36.

The 28 stands for the percentage of your monthly income that most banks will allow you to allocate to housing. This includes the total sum of everything from mortgage payments to insurance, property taxes, and homeowner's dues (if applicable). If your annual income is $60,000 and your monthly income is $5,000, you can allocate 28 percent, or $1,400, to total monthly housing costs. Depending on the prevailing interest rate, the bank will calculate the size of loan it feels comfortable extending.

But then there's the 36 part of the deal, which refers to the maximum percentage of your monthly income that the bank will permit for *all* debt that you regularly make payments on, including credit cards, car loans, alimony, child support, and any other longer-term financial responsibilities. (A longer-term loan is generally considered to be one that will take you more than six months to pay off.)

So even though the initial 28 percent calculation might allow you to allocate $1,400 per month to your housing costs, the fact that you are carrying credit card debt plus a car loan that together require you to pay $700 a month changes the equation. Of your $5,000 monthly income, you can allocate only $1,800 to all recurring debt. After you subtract the $700 you pay each month even if you don't have a house, you are left with $1,100 for housing. The amount of your bank loan will reflect this number.

Types of Mortgages

D ecades ago, it was a lot simpler to choose a mortgage, because the options were so much more limited. Almost everyone got loans that were paid back over 30 years and for which fixed percentages of interest were charged. But now a whole range of choices is available to borrowers, and entire books have been written analyzing the possibilities. All the same, you can generally divide mortgages into two basic types, based on how the interest you pay is calculated:

■ **Fixed rate mortgages (FRMs).** All mortgages used be *fixed rate*, which means that the interest rate stayed constant throughout the life of the loan. That meant no surprises: you knew what you would be paying every month for the next 30 years. Some people still prefer to go with fixed-rate loans precisely because of their predictability: No matter what is happening to interest rates in the marketplace, your monthly payments will be the same.

■ **Adjustable rate mortgages (ARMs).** The opposite of a fixed rate mortgage is an adjustable rate mortgage (called an ARM and also known as a *variable rate mortgage*) where the interest rate varies with the prevailing interest rate in the marketplace. Depending on the terms of the loan, the interest rate being charged could change from month to month (in the case of a "fully adjustable" loan) or every 6 or 12 months. This means that your monthly mortgage could go either up or down at the end of each designated period. The state of the market determines the direction. When interest rates in general

INSIDER'S INSIGHT

Length of Mortgage

" Keep in mind that, unless there's a prepayment penalty, you can always speed up payments of a 30-year loan, but you can't slow down payment of a 15-year loan. "

Lovinda Beal, Agent,
Cornish & Carey,
Portola Valley, California

go up, your mortgage payments will increase. When interest rates go down, your mortgage payments will decrease.

Basic ARM terms

Here's a list of the basic words and phrases used to describe the characteristics of an ARM.

TERM	DEFINITION
Adjustment period	The amount of time that must pass between adjustments on the interest rate for an ARM. Typically, the period is 6 months or 1 year.
Initial rate	The starting interest rate for an ARM. At the end of the contracted period for the initial rate, the interest rate will be adjusted based on the stated adjustment period and on changes in the specified financial index.
Financial index	To calculate mortgage payments for ARMs, the loans are tied to an "index," which is the interest rate as calculated in a particular way by a particular organization. ARMs can be tied to any one of a variety of indices, including but not limited to the Constant Maturity Treasury Index, the 11th District Cost of Funds Index, and the London Inter Bank Offering Rates. Your loan contract will specify which index your mortgage is tied to.
Margin	This refers to the bank's profit margin above the value of the financial index being used. The bank seeks to make a profit above the costs of inflation. The index is a measure of the cost of funds as measured by inflation.
Maximum rate	The maximum interest rate that a bank can charge on a specific adjustable rate loan. This rate varies from loan to loan.
Rate adjustment cap	The limits of how much the interest rate may increase or decrease on an ARM for a specific adjustment period.

There are many other types of loans, although they are all based on the two prime distinctions between fixed and variable interest rates. Five of the most common:

■ **Hybrid loans.** These are a cross between fixed and adjustable rate mortgages. Initially resembling fixed loans—they stay at the same interest rate for a pre-determined period of time, from as little as one year to as long as ten years—they then convert to ARMs, generally at the prevailing interest rate. Hybrid loans are the most popular type of mortgages today.

■ **Balloon mortgages.** These are like hybrid loans in the sense that they start out at a fixed rate for a certain amount of time. The exact time is negotiable, but it can range from four to ten years. The resemblance stops there, because the entire balance (the "balloon") of the loan is due at the end of this time. You should consider a balloon loan only if you desperately want to purchase a property and are absolutely confident that you will be able to refinance it before the balloon is due—or you are certain that you will have more than enough money to cover the entire loan before that time.

■ **Interest-only loans.** These are just what they sound like—your monthly mortgage payments are applied only to the interest on your loan. This means that the amount you owe does not decrease over time. In a market where houses are increasing in value, you will still build equity—sometimes quite a bit of equity—in your property, but in slower markets you may not. You may even end up owing the bank more than your property is worth. However, if you are short on cash, this is a good way to bootstrap your way into a home you otherwise couldn't afford. And unless your loan has a prepayment penalty, nothing prevents you from paying back part of the mortgage when you have some spare cash.

INSIDER'S INSIGHT

Relationships Are Key

To find a good broker or lender, depend on relationships. Ask your Realtor who he or she recommends. That broker or lender, because they want to maintain the relationship, will be much more accountable than if you found a broker or lender through a mass mailing or telemarketing.

Scott Brader,
Branch Manager and BBB member,
Colony Mortgage, Westerville, Ohio

■ **Negative amortization loans.** A riskier way to go is a negative amortization loan. In this type of mortgage, your monthly payment doesn't even cover the interest rate. The amount you owe actually increases each month, so that your loan gets bigger, not smaller, as time goes by. Use this type of loan *only* if you have excellent reasons to believe that your finances will change for the better in the future (or that the property is going to appreciate significantly over the next few years). In most cases, those opting for a negative amortization loan plan to refinance and acquire a standard loan as soon as they are able to afford higher monthly payments.

■ **Subprime loans.** People with poor credit used to have difficulty breaking into the housing market. That is no longer the case. Even if you have less-than-stellar credit, you can probably still get a loan. But there's a catch: you will be offered terms less favorable than those given to people with good credit. A subprime loan is a mortgage that charges higher interest than the competitive going rate—typically 0.1 percent to 0.6 percent higher. It is specifically targeted to people who can't get a loan any other way. Some people accept subprime loans in order to create a record of prompt payments that lifts their credit score. This then allows them to refinance at some later date on better terms.

What to look for in a mortgage

When you start shopping for an ARM, you will hear of loans with starting interest rates that are well below market. Investigate such loans very carefully. They are offering what the mortgage industry calls "teaser" rates—low rates that entice you to you to sign up for a particular loan. It's not long before the rates rise—typically within 6 to 12 months, but sometimes even sooner.

More important that the initial rate are two other components of the loan: the index and the margin:

- **Index.** This is the measure on which the bank bases your interest rate, and it is based on a publicly published financial index such as the 11th District Cost of Funds Index. Adjustable rate mortgages are usually tied to the average interest rate that the bank pays on six-month CDs.

- **Margin.** This is the profit margin on the money that the banker intends to lend you. Although most margins are between 2 percent and 3 percent, they can be higher if you have bad credit. The exact margin depends on the lender and the type of loan. The lower the bank's margin, the better the deal will be for you. The amount of the margin should be clearly written in your contract. Make sure you understand what the margin is before committing to a loan. If you have good credit and it's above 3 percent, take your business elsewhere.

The Three Most Common Types of Mortgages

TYPE OF MORTGAGE	ADVANTAGES	DISADVANTAGES
Fixed	Your monthly payment is predictable. You can lock in a good interest rate for the duration of the loan.	If interest rates fall, you're stuck with an expensive loan. There's frequently a prepayment penalty. Interest rates tend to be higher than for adjustable rate mortgages (ARMs).
Adjustable	Interest rates are lower than fixed. If interest rates fall, your monthly mortgage payment decreases.	If interest rates rise, your monthly mortgage payment increases. Your monthly payments may fluctuate beyond your control, and in worst-case scenarios, you might not be able to afford the increased sums due.
Hybrid	Your monthly payment is predictable for a substantial period of time. You can lock in a good interest rate for years. After that point, if the interest rate falls, your payments will decrease.	You haven't locked in a favorable rate for the duration of the loan. If interest rates rise after the initial term, your payments will increase.

15 or 30?

One of the most important choices you'll make when deciding on a loan is picking the *length* of the loan. You'll most often have to select between a 15- and a 30-year mortgage (although sometimes loans of other lengths are available).

The chief advantages of a 15-year mortgage are that you pay significantly less interest over the lifetime of the loan and you pay off the loan in half the time of the 30-year option. The chief disadvantage: the monthly payments are higher.

The advantages and disadvantages of a 30-year mortgage are exactly the inverse of this. You pay more interest over the life of the loan, and it takes a lot longer to be free from your mortgage. On the other hand, the payments on a 30-year mortgage are lower than on a 15-year loan, leaving you with more spare cash in the near term.

First-time home buyers might not have much choice. Given the fact that your home-buying process is driven so much by available cash—the amount you can spare for the down payment—a 30-year mortgage might provide the only way to get a big enough mortgage for the house of your dreams. Indeed, it's very rare for first-time home buyers to opt for the 15-year option. Some are even taking out 35- and 40-year mortgages.

Using a mortgage broker

Traditionally, banks and other lending institutions worked directly with home buyers to arrange for loans. But as the types of mortgages have become more varied and complex, mortgage brokers have become much more popular. Today more than 80 percent of the mortgages in the United States are negotiated by mortgage brokers. (In most states, mortgage brokers are regulated in order to protect consumers.)

Engaging a mortgage broker to work on your behalf can help you during the home-buying process. Think of it as having a personal mortgage shopper: a broker has relationships with a range of lenders, understands the different loans offered by each one, and can give you advice on the best match for you.

If you have a poor or nonexistent credit history, a broker could make the difference between getting and not getting a mortgage. It's a broker's business to be familiar with the different types of programs and loans available for people in special circumstances.

A mortgage broker performs a number of key functions:

- Evaluates your particular financial situation. This includes getting copies of your credit report and income tax returns in order to determine the size and type of loan you will qualify for.

- Reviews the market to find a mortgage that fits your particular needs. In addition to presenting you with your options—and, in the best circumstances, explaining the pros and cons of your various choices—a broker will facilitate the whole process so you never have to deal directly with the lender.

■ Helps you get preapproved for a loan if you haven't already been preapproved (see page 51). Although many first-time buyers become prequalified by going directly to the lenders themselves, some prefer to begin working with a mortgage broker early in the process. In general, because a broker's job is to make the whole process easier for you, the sooner you find one that you feel comfortable with, the further ahead in the game you'll be.

■ Compiles all necessary documentation that the lender requires.

■ Helps you complete the lender application form and submits it to the lender for processing.

Brokers are regulated by 17 federal laws (and counting), numerous regulations, and dozens of state laws and licensing boards. The primary goal of these regulations is to educate consumers and make the terms of various loans they will choose from more transparent. Many of these regulations are specifically focused on disclosing the risks of "nontraditional" mortgages, which include adjustable rate mortgages (ARMs) that come with low initial "teaser" rates, interest-only loans, negative amortization loans, and "stated income" loans that don't verify income or assets.

Second Mortgages and Seller Carry Backs

Because first-time home buyers are often strapped for cash, it's not uncommon for them to take out a second or even third mortgage to cover the down payment. In effect, they are financing 100 percent of the cost of the home. And there are many first-time home-buying programs at the city, county, and state level that will provide additional mortgages. Employers and builders of new homes can also offer mortgages.

The seller can also "carry back" some of the cost of the property. In such cases, you are in effect borrowing money from the seller, and you pay that amount back with interest, just as you would for a traditional mortgage. The advantage to sellers of agreeing to do this is that they can sell the house more quickly, or for better terms, than they would otherwise be able to do. In hot seller's markets, it's rare to see sellers agreeing to carry back. But in a buyer's market, sellers are more willing to negotiate.

QUICK TIP

Nurture Your Broker Relationship

If you get a good mortgage broker—one who explains things clearly, lays out your options, helps you get the best deal, and streamlines the red tape—keep in touch! As with any professional relationship, you should always be thinking of the future. So when it's time to refinance, get an equity line, or purchase your next property, you've already got someone in your corner.

Your Cash Outlay

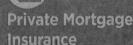

Private Mortgage Insurance

Private Mortgage Insurance (PMI) is insurance that you buy to protect the lender in case you default on your loan. If you can't put down the full 20 percent down payment, your lender will require PMI, which could add between $200 and $1,000 annually to the cost of your mortgage. As you pay down the amount of your mortgage—or your property appreciates in value—you will be able to cancel your PMI. The Homeowners Protection Act of 1998 requires PMI to be canceled when the amount owed on the mortgage is less than 78 percent of the value of the home.

A t this point it's time to take serious stock of your available financial resources. That's the cold hard cash you can put your hands on. Although you will be borrowing most of the money you need for purchasing your home, you will still need cash in order to successfully complete the deal. Depending on your circumstances and the home you buy, you may need significant amounts of cash. You won't have to shell out this money just yet—but you will have to understand precisely how much you have to work with.

The down payment

A down payment is the portion of the purchase price you have to pay to the seller in order to get the loan. Your lender wants to make sure you have a significant investment in the property so that you will be motivated to pay off the loan. If you can't pay your mortgage, you would not only have to give the property back, you would also lose your down payment money—which could range from thousands to hundreds of thousands of dollars. The bank wants to make it as difficult as possible for you to walk away from the loan.

Most first-time home buyers find that their home-buying decisions depend as much on how much cash they have available for a down payment as on what kind of monthly mortgage payments they can afford. One of the prime motivations for buying a home is that your mortgage payments wouldn't be that much more than your monthly rent.

In such cases, the only thing standing between you and a home of your own is the down payment.

You'll need to actually hand over the down payment at the time that you "close" on the property (see page 162). And the check you write at that time will also include a number of other "closing costs" (see pages 166-168). So you'll need a significant amount of cash above the price of the down payment in order to complete the home-buying transaction.

Traditionally, a standard down payment was 20 percent of the cost of the property. But as housing prices soared, this percentage priced many first-time home buyers out of the market. Twenty percent of the average $150,000 mortgage is $30,000. So in recent years, many lenders have begun to accept smaller amounts: 10 percent, 5 percent, or even less. There are even special programs for first-time home buyers that allow them to purchase a house with a greatly reduced down payment—and sometimes with no down payment at all! According to the National Association of Realtors (NAR), the average first-time home buyer offers a down payment of just 2 percent.

This is possible because there are any number of special loans that require a very low—or no—down payment at all. A first-time home buyer might even get a second mortgage to pay for the 20 percent down payment on the first mortgage.

Although it may seem that the lower the down payment you can offer, the better, there are other factors to consider. First and foremost, the lower your down payment, the higher the loan you will need to get—and the more you'll have to pay each month in principal and interest.

Second, having less than a 20 percent down payment means that most lenders will require Private Mortgage Insurance (PMI) that protects them in case you have to forfeit the loan for any reason.

Help with Your Credit Rating?

With all the publicity about identity theft and credit report errors, you might find yourself attracted to one of the numerous services (usually advertising on the Internet or late-night television) promising to get you a free copy of your credit report and help you clear up any problems. Treat these offers with caution. You are already entitled to one free credit report at least annually and can get it by going to one of the three U.S. credit bureaus (see page 67) or to this—and only this—web-site: *www.annualcreditreport.com*. There's no need to go through an intermediary. Usually such companies have something to sell, and the quality and credibility of such offers varies widely. Check out any company with the Better Business Bureau before giving any personal information—especially your social security number.

Pulling Together the Down Payment

Many first-time home buyers don't have sufficient cash to purchase the house of their dreams. They have two choices: put off buying until they can save up the down payment or turn to other sources of funds. Some people have relatives or friends who are more than happy to give their loved ones a boost into their first home. In most cases, banks won't allow you to borrow the amount of your down payment. Instead, they will require the donor to sign a letter stating the money is a gift, not a loan.

Borrowing from a 401K is another common way for aspiring home-owners to obtain the down payment for their first home. The only cost is the interest you forgo as a result of not having the funds in your 401K account. However, substantial risk is involved in taking this route. If you change jobs, you must pay back the loan within an amount of time speci-fied by your employer. Usually that is 60 to 90 days. If you can't pay it back within that time, the transac-tion is treated like a withdrawal rather than a borrowing of funds, and you'll run up against some very hefty penalties and taxes.

Two of the main sources of no or very low down payment loans for first-time home buyers are Fannie Mae and the FHA (Federal Housing Authority):

- **Federal National Mortgage Association** (commonly known as Fannie Mae) (*www.fanniemae.com*). Founded in 1938 by the federal government, Fannie Mae is a share-holder-owned company that works with lenders to offer special loans and services that help low-, moderate-, and middle-income families own their own homes.

- **Federal Housing Authority** (FHA) (*http://www.hud. gov/fha/*) was set up as part of the New Deal in 1934. It guarantees private home mortgages (FHA loans) and provides funds to promote housing construction, espe-cially for lower-income people. By insuring mortgages, FHA allows lenders to work with borrowers even if they have some credit problems, have filed bankruptcy, or possess higher than average debt-to-income ratios.

Beyond the down payment

Take into account other expenses you'll accrue before you get the keys in your hands. Many loans have *points* associ-ated with them (see page 63). You'll have other closing costs, such as deed and title insurance (see pages 166-168). And many lenders will want to see that you have sufficient cash in a savings account—or other liquid assets—to cover two or three months of mortgage payments.

Other costs vary from lender to lender and from mortgage to mortgage. Some charge for application and/or process-ing costs. These can range from $50 to $500—and can sometimes be avoided simply by asking the lender to waive them. Usually the bank will charge you for obtaining the most current version of your credit report—that's another $35 to $60. And then there's the fee for the appraiser, who your bank hires to verify the market value of the property in question. That fee ranges from $200 to $600, depending on the value of the home and the geographic region.

A bank needs to profit from the loans it makes—and it will do so in any number of ways, including margins, points, interest, and other fees. If a mortgage seems too good to be true, it might well be. Make sure you understand all the terms of a particular loan before you sign on the dotted line.

Points

A point is advance interest on your mortgage. Charging you for points is a way for the lender to recoup some of the costs of processing your loan application. (Like mortgage interest, points are deductible on your income tax.)

One point is 1 percent of the total amount you are financing. Two points are 2 percent, and so on. So if a bank is charging you 1.5 points for a $100,000 loan, you pay $1,500 upon securing that mortgage.

In general, if you choose a fixed-rate loan (see page 53), there is an inverse relationship between the number of points you pay and the long-term interest rate of your loan. A no-point loan might have a 5 percent interest rate, whereas a 2-point loan would offer a 4.5 percent interest rate.

Deciding between a points or non-points loan often comes down to two factors: how much ready cash you have and how long you expect to stay in your home. The less money you have available—and the less time you plan to own your home—the more a no-points loan makes sense, even though your monthly mortgage payments will be higher. On the other hand, if you plan to be in your home for many years, it may be preferable to pay points in exchange for the lower interest rate in the long term.

Property Taxes

Your property taxes are based on the value of the property. The "assessment" of how much your property is worth—and therefore how much you will pay in annual taxes—is made by your local city or county. Depending on your local tax authority, you may pay your property taxes annually or bi-annually. The rate at which you are taxed can vary considerably from county to county or even city to city. Before you make an offer on a house, make sure you can afford to pay the property taxes.

Get It in Writing

Make sure your lender gives you an accounting of all fees *in writing* before you sign the loan contract. The last thing you want is to find out that you don't have enough cash to close on the deal—or, worse, that the lifetime cost of the mortgage is many thousands of dollars higher than you expected it to be. Lenders are required by law to show within 72 hours of approving a loan a detailed "good faith" estimate of what the costs will be. When the loan is actually handed over at closing, however, buyers should carefully check this estimate against the actual costs. And let the buyer beware: despite the legal requirement to do so, many brokers don't provide the initial breakdown in fees and may need to be pushed to do so.

Your monthly housing expenses

Once you've figured out how much cash you'll need up front, it's time to do some more calculations. This time you'll be figuring out what your actual monthly cash outlay will be on your new home. After all, it's not just the size of the monthly mortgage payments that determines whether you can afford a house. A number of other expenses come into play, including homeowner's insurance, property taxes, maintenance, and association dues (if you choose a condo or gated community).

Your Monthly Housing Expenses

Use this worksheet to calculate your monthly housing expenses. Your agent can give you estimates for property taxes and insurance premiums for your particular region.

COMPONENT	COST
Monthly mortgage payment	_____
Property taxes (divide by 12 to get per-month cost)	_____
Annual homeowner's insurance premiums (divide by 12)	_____
Maintenance (calculate 3 percent of home price and divide by 12)	_____
Monthly association dues	_____
Other expenses	_____
Total monthly cash outlay	_____

Are You a Good Bet for a Mortgage?

Will a bank feel comfortable lending a large sum of money, often several hundred thousand dollars, to you? The answer depends on your credit report and your credit score.

A *credit report* is created by a credit reporting agency and provides a record of all your creditors—current and past—and your payment history. This list includes information from banks (if, for instance, you had a car loan), credit card companies, student loan departments, auto credit cards, or any other business that extended you credit for products or services. Credit reports give banks information about whether you are the type of person who will likely pay your bills on time and thus are likely to repay a mortgage and make your payments at the agreed-upon times.

In addition to your credit report, you also have a *credit score*—a three-digit number that is key to determining what type of mortgage you will get. This number is a distillation of all the data found in your credit history. The credit agency assigns points to various aspects of your borrowing behavior and comes up with a single number, which can range from 300 to 850. The higher the number, the better

INSIDER'S INSIGHT

Surprises in Your Credit Report

I'd say that 75 percent of people are surprised by something in their credit report. That's why I advise you to get your credit report as soon as possible so you have time to clear up any problems. Often times a lender will work with you to try and correct any errors or provide adequate explanations of anything that drags down your rating.

Cristy Shaw, Broker Associate, Keller Williams Realty, Orange Beach, Alabama

your credit. As of 2006, the average credit score in the U.S. was approximately 650. Above that, you have a good chance of securing a loan at the prime rate. Below that, you may have to accept a loan with a higher rate of interest.

The score is based largely upon your payment history. But other factors affect it as well, including the total amount of your outstanding debt, the type of credit you currently have, and the length of time you've had credit extended to you.

What your credit report and score say about you is critical. But a surprisingly large number of people have no idea what their credit rating or score is until they apply for a mortgage. It's a good idea to check your credit *before* the bank does to give yourself a chance to correct any errors or prepare an explanation that might change your lender's assessment of your situation.

FICO Scores

FICO stands for "Fair Isaac Corporation," the company that provides the standard credit score calculation model in the United States. The score is calculated using a mathematical formula developed by FICO, and it is supposed to predict the likelihood of a borrower defaulting on a loan.

Although the exact formula for generating your FICO score is confidential, FICO has made some details public:

- 35% depends on whether you have paid bills on time.

- 30% depends on the "capacity" of your current available credit—such as credit card limits and lines of credit. For example, if you have a credit card balance of $500 on a card that will allow you $1,000 of credit, your capacity is 50 percent.

- 15% is based on how long you've had a credit history. In other words, the time since you were issued your first credit card.

- 10% is based on the type of credit you use.

- 10% is based on the amount of credit you've recently applied for and been granted.

A FICO score is usually between 300 and 850, with the median being 725.

There's also a new way of scoring—called the Vantage Score—and it is now being offered by all three major credit bureaus, Equifax, Experian, and Trans Union. Instead of a numerical grade, you get a letter grade, from A down to F.

Who creates credit reports?

There are three major credit reference agencies in the United States that give out your credit history to current or prospective creditors and employers:

Equifax

http://equifax.com
P.O. Box 105873
Atlanta, GA 30348
1-800-685-1111

Experian

http://experian.com
P.O. Box 2002
Allen, TX 75013
Consumer Credit Questions
1-888-397-3742

Trans Union

http://www.tuc.com
Post Office Box 2000
Chester, PA 19022
1-800-888-4213

These agencies *collect* information; they don't create it. They don't make judgments about whether or not you get a loan; they simply provide data to the bank or lending institution, which then makes the decision based on that information.

The easiest way to obtain your credit reports is to go directly to the credit agencies themselves. All three of the main agencies have websites where you can order your report. In many states, they are legally required to provide you with a free copy of your credit report once a year. You can also visit *www.annualcreditreport.com*.

Bad Credit?

Perhaps you missed a credit card payment or were late paying back a student loan. These things can come back to haunt you when you apply for a loan. Even if you slipped up just once or twice a few years ago, it can show up in your credit report and reflect upon your credit rating. You can send an explanation of 100 words or less to any credit agency, outlining any special or extenuating circumstances that led to these black marks on your report. What you say will become part of your permanent record.

If you find errors in your credit report, straighten them out before applying for a loan. By law, if you notify the credit agency in writing of a problem, it must be resolved within 30 days, and any disputed or unconfirmed information must be deleted. If that occurs, make sure that the agency sends out the revised credit report to all potential creditors who received the erroneous report within the last six months.

Sometimes your only choice is to accept a loan that has a higher interest rate or less favorable terms than if you had excellent credit. Consider this an opportunity to improve your credit. After all, there are few things that will increase your score over time as much as being a reliable and prompt payer of a mortgage!

Yield Spread Premiums

Yield Spread Premiums (YSP) are cash rebates paid to mortgage brokers by lenders when they sell a loan with an interest rate above the wholesale rate that the borrower has qualified for. Mortgage brokers are required to disclose YSP as a fee that is paid outside closing (POC).

YSPs themselves are not a problem: they are a standard means of reimbursing mortgage brokers for their services. But they can be excessive and not disclosed until the last minute—at closing—which frequently puts them in the category of predatory lending practices.

The Center for Responsible Lending says that brokers need to disclose YSP fully up front before a borrower commits to a loan—when they "lock in" the rate. This way, a borrower can make sure the broker is not charging them a higher interest rate than they actually qualify for, given their credit history.

Predatory lending

Predatory lending is the practice of using illegal or unethical behavior in order to reap unreasonable profit from a mortgage transaction. Predatory lending includes deceptive marketing, failure to disclose all terms related to a loan, and falsifying documents. According to the Center for Responsible Lending (*www.responsiblelending.org*), there are distinct warning signs of predatory lending:

- **Junk fees.** Be wary of excessive fees that are absorbed into the body of the loan. Because they become part of the loan, they are easy to overlook. Especially watch out for "loan application" or "loan processing" fees that raise the total fee to more than 2 percent of the mortgage amount. Assume that anything over that percentage is suspect and demand to know precisely why you are being charged for each line item.

- **Unreasonable prepayment penalties.** Some mortgages have what are called "prepayment penalties," which are fees for paying off the loan early—before the 15- or 30-year term is up. This can be a problem, especially if you have an ARM and interest rates drop and you want to refinance or sell your home before the term is up. Unreasonable penalties include restrictions on prepayment for four years or more after closing on the loan and prepayment penalties that add up to more than five or six months' worth of interest.

- **Kickbacks to brokers.** This occurs when a broker convinces a home buyer to accept a higher interest rate than the market currently offers in return for a cash bonus from the lender.

- **Unnecessary products or services.** Some lenders will try to sell you superfluous insurance or other products or services, such as credit insurance, along with the loan.

- **Mandatory arbitration.** If your loan says that you must submit to "mandatory arbitration," treat it with care. It means that you are not allowed to take your lender to court later if you find out they've engaged in predatory practices.

- **Steering.** Predatory lenders do something called "steering," which is encouraging a borrower to accept a subprime mortgage when they might have qualified for a loan with more competitive rates. According to Fannie Mae, as many as 50 percent of borrowers who signed up for subprime mortgages could have qualified for loans with more favorable terms. Before you commit to a subprime loan, always shop around.

QUICK TIP

You Always Pay the Piper

Don't be fooled by the so-called "no closing cost" loan. Although you are not required to pay cash out of pocket at closing for the normal closing costs, the lender typically includes the closing costs in the principal balance or charges a higher interest rate in order to cover the advance of closing costs.

Market Watch

"*When interest rates start to go up or down and market dynamics begin to change, it can really confuse people. The first thing you want to do is a market analysis to see what's happening out there. That way, you'll make sure you don't overpay for a property.*"

Nancy Bristow,
Emerald Coast Realty,
Pensacola, Florida

Investigate *the* Market

The Economic Landscape

Y ou've prequalified for a mortgage, defined your wants and needs, narrowed down your choice of neighborhoods, and chosen an agent. Now it's time to investigate the particulars of the market you're facing.

First, consider whether you're in a buyer's or a seller's market. These terms are used by real estate professionals as shorthand for summarizing a number of key economic factors that make a difference to home pricing and availability. Those factors range from the prevailing interest rates and the strength of the local economy to rates of employment, inflation, and available housing stock.

QUICK TIP

Surviving a Seller's Market

When bidding wars are common, you can increase the chances that your offer will be accepted by:

■ **Putting more money down**. A low down payment could hurt you in a bidding war. That's because, if in doubt, a seller will choose the offer that has the least chance of hitting a snag during closing. Offers with low or no down payment mortgages have a much higher risk of being rejected by sellers than those with even 10 percent down.

■ **Reducing "conditions" you insist upon before agreeing to buy a particular property.** The more a seller has to change or fix up a property before you'll accept it, the less likely they will be to consider your offer.

■ **Including a buyer's intro letter.** Sometimes writing a heartfelt letter and including personal references is the best way to win the heart of a seller. Leaving a home is often an emotional experience, and many property owners want to make sure that their house will be in good hands. Assuring them that you will take care of their beloved property can often make the difference between acceptance and rejection.

Buyer's markets

If you're fortunate, you'll be looking for a house when there are more houses for sale than people to buy them. When supply outstrips demand, there is generally a much wider range of choices, as well as lower prices. Not only are there are more houses to choose from, they stay on the market longer. You'll have an opportunity to view a much broader range of properties, and their prices will often be negotiable. Sellers are likely to throw in extras, like window coverings, appliances, and even furniture. Contractors are more likely to have free time when the real estate market is sluggish, so if there is work to be done on the house, they will provide more competitive bids. Buying during a downturn can also mean that your equity will rise more rapidly once the market recovers.

Although a buyer's market generally means excellent news for first time buyers, there are some potential downsides. Such markets tend to occur during times of greater economic uncertainty or risk. Frequently, interest rates are high—or expected to rise—which means you can afford less home than you would if rates were lower or declining. The local economy might be in trouble. Your region's workforce could be experiencing a general downsizing that could make your own employment situation uncertain.

Beware of Rising Rates

Although a buyer's market might seem like nirvana—after all, you'll have a great selection of properties to choose from, and sellers may be throwing in freebies right and left—one of the chief causes of a buyer's market is the threat of rising interest rates. If you plan to use an adjustable rate mortgage in order to get the biggest bang for your housing buck, be aware that your monthly payments may rise quickly. You will want to be conservative when it comes to estimating housing costs.

QUICK TIP

Time Out

Take note of how long properties have been on the market. If the average time a house in your area spends on the market is short—a month or less—you are facing a seller's market. Move quickly if you see something you like. If, on the other hand, properties are lingering on the market for months, you are probably in a buyer's market and it will be easier for you to negotiate price and terms to your advantage.

INSIDER'S INSIGHT

Raising Your "Earnest Money"

In addition to putting down a larger down payment for your mortgage, the bigger the earnest money—or the cash you give to the seller when you sign the contract—the better for you in a seller's market. You might think the seller will get his or her money regardless, but putting down 5 percent rather than 2 percent or 3 percent will prove to them that you really want the property, and could be the deciding factor in a bidding war.

J.D. Songstad, Realtor, RE/Max Westside Properties, Los Angeles, California

Seller's markets

When there are fewer properties available than people who want to buy homes, you're in a seller's market. Prices tend to be higher—in some cases, much higher—and buyers can find themselves in bidding wars, which force them to make offers far above the asking prices.

When demand for properties exceeds supply, sellers also get pickier about other aspects of the offers they receive. They accept fewer requests for fixing problems, insist on closing conditions that suit their own convenience, refuse to negotiate on improvements or other conditions, and are less flexible about accommodating buyers.

Why are so many people eager to buy during seller's markets? For one thing, interest rates might be low during a seller's market, allowing people to afford much larger or more luxurious houses than they could otherwise hope for. General economic conditions might also be a factor: if employment rates are high and wages rising, a general feeling of prosperity might cause more people to think about owning their own homes.

In rapidly appreciating markets, real estate is viewed as a prime—even indispensable—investment. In the early to mid-2000s, for instance, double-digit annual increases in the value of real estate caused large numbers of first-time buyers to flood the market, eager to reap the financial rewards of home ownership and fearful that they would miss out if they didn't purchase immediately.

Open Season

The *season* in which you buy a house can make a big difference to the price you pay. In general, housing sales—and prices—are lowest at the beginning and end of each calendar year and highest in the summer. Sales tend to increase through the spring, peak in June or July, and begin declining in early fall.

These price fluctuations are the result of a combination of weather and holiday and school schedules. Few people choose to move during the winter holidays, which are usually packed with activities. Parents don't want to disrupt their children during the school year, so they don't list—or look at—properties until spring. That way they can move during summer vacation.

And properties just *look* better during certain seasons. It can be difficult for sellers to make even the most delightful property seem enticing in the middle of a blizzard. So many put off listing their homes until the weather improves.

Leverage these seasonal trends to your advantage. Consider shopping for a new home during "off" seasons to get a break on price. Sellers who put properties on the market in the dead of winter probably have no choice: perhaps their work requires them to move to a different city, or there might be a divorce or other compelling reason to sell the property in February instead of May. By shopping out of season, you can sometimes get a good price on a property that would normally be out of your budget.

It's true that the size of the housing inventory is often limited during off-peak seasons. But being flexible about timing can work in your favor, especially in highly competitive seller's markets.

INSIDER'S INSIGHT

Preparing Yourself for a Seller's Market

It's important for buyers to prepare themselves emotionally for a tough market. In 2005, for example, there was no inventory at all, and interest rates were low, so everyone was buying, making it hard for first-time buyers. They have to be ready to jump on anything they like, and to be realistic about what they can get.

Kenneth Etter,
Broker and BBB member,
Kenneth Etter Realty, Reno, Nevada

What's Available

A lthough you might have mapped out your wants and needs, determined your perfect neighborhood, prequalified for a loan, and worked out a realistic budget, unfortunately none of that will matter one whit if no properties are available in your area or price range. Performing a detailed survey of the available housing inventory in your chosen area *before* you start looking at specific properties will help you to be realistic about your options. This way you'll avoid wasting time and effort considering properties that are out of your reach. To learn what's out there:

■ **Use the Internet.** According to a 2005 survey by the National Association of Realtors, more than 85 percent of home buyers used the Internet during some phase of the home-buying process. An Internet search can bring you information on everything from the number of properties currently on the market to which ones were sold recently and at what prices. You can also view the details of properties currently on the market and search for homes with specific attributes, such as number of bedrooms, bathrooms, size of lot, or price. Some sites offer "virtual tours" of available properties so you can walk through them from your desk. (See pages 80-81 for more on using the Internet.)

■ **Tour targeted neighborhoods.** Revisit your targeted neighborhoods looking for "for sale," "sale pending," and "sold" signs. Write down the addresses, the listing agents' names, phone numbers, and websites.

■ **Read local papers.** Check the real estate section daily for data on the state of your chosen market. You can get a sense of how the market is performing and what you can expect to pay for a property in your desired location.

■ **Review the Multiple Listing Service (MLS) listings.** The MLS is one of the most powerful tools you have for understanding what is happening in a specific market. Once you have signed up with an agent, they will review the properties listed on the relevant MLS with you to give you a sense of what the current market inventory is like. Most real estate agents will then monitor the MLS actively on your behalf and let you know when new properties become available. Some agents will email those listings to you; others will let you access limited views of the MLS via their websites.

■ **Ask around.** The more you network, the more information you'll gather. Check in with friends, relatives, co-workers, and acquaintances for information about the local housing market that might otherwise be "under the radar." Give your email address to anyone you trust who might have information about purchasing a home in a desired locale.

■ **Pick up free real estate magazines.** These are an excellent resource for viewing the prevailing prices and features of houses in particular locations

Open Houses

Visiting open houses is one of the smartest things you can do when getting serious about buying your first home. An open house gives you a first-hand look at what's out there. You can walk around and actually see, touch, feel, smell, and hear what it would be like to live in a particular property.

Attending open houses will give you a more realistic picture of housing prices and leave you better prepared when it comes time to make an offer on a property. You can find open house listings in the newspapers serving the areas you're interested in. Look for small neighborhood publications rather than giant metropolitan dailies.

What Is an MLS?

A Multiple Listing Service, or MLS, is an online database that allows real estate agents who represent the sellers of properties to share information with agents representing buyers. Rather than just providing the particulars of properties listed by a single agent, an MLS combines the listings of multiple agents. Using an MLS, an agent can quickly and easily retrieve information about all homes for sale in a given area or price range, rather than having to separately investigate the inventory of individual listing agents.

There is no single MLS system, but a multitude of such systems across the country. An MLS may be owned and operated by a real estate company, a county or regional real estate Board or Association of Realtors, or a trade association.

Most MLS systems restrict access to licensed agents who are members of a local Board or Association of Realtors and are members of the trade association. Someone selling their own home cannot put a listing for their property into the MLS.

Depending on the rules of the MLS in question, agents might be able to make all the listed properties available on their websites, or they might be restricted to displaying only the properties they've listed themselves. Many agents require Internet visitors to register online before they can get access to MLS listings. Although such registration is free, it usually results in a sales email or call from the agent in question—which can be helpful or intrusive, depending on where you are in the house-hunting process and whether you are looking for an agent to help you find a house.

Real Estate Decoder

Real estate ads are full of cryptic descriptions that seem to be written in a foreign language. A key to some common acronyms and abbreviations:

ABBREVIATION	DEFINITION
BR	Bedroom
BA	Bathroom
LR	Living Room
DR	Dining Room
FR	Family Room
AC	Air Conditioning
BSMT or BMENT	Basement
FP	Fireplace
MOL	More or less (refers to size of house or lot)
AEK	All electric kitchen
HW	Hardwood floors
DW	Dishwasher
TLC	Tender loving care
BOM	Back on market

Using the Internet

The Internet has opened up a whole new world of home-buying help. To understand what was going on in a particular market, buyers used to be dependent on real estate agents or what they could glean from driving through neighborhoods and scanning the local papers. Now with just a click of the mouse, you can find out nearly everything you need to know about a given agent, neighborhood, or property.

The biggest problem you will have is that of too much information. Just about every professional involved in helping people buy or sell houses now has a website. Some of these sites are little more than "electronic calling cards" that provide agent bios and contact information. But many are vibrant, interactive marketplaces. They can offer links to mortgage lenders, brokers, and appraisers, as well as mortgage calculators and application forms for a credit report, plus search engines that allow you to find properties that meet your particular needs.

In addition to agents' own websites, the number of independent sites that offer real estate information keeps proliferating. A handful of especially useful ones:

■ **Realtor.com** (*www.realtor.com*) is the granddaddy of all real estate sites, run by the National Association of Realtors (NAR). This site is notable for its comprehensive, searchable database of properties for sale, where you can enter your desired city, state, and price range and other features, such as the number of bedrooms and bathrooms. You can also get reports from agents with information on the market activity in their particular areas. You can do a search on mortgage rates and find a lender, a broker, or an appraiser.

■ **MSN Real Estate** (*http://realestate.msn.com*) provides you with a host of tools to explore buying, selling, renting, and renovating properties in neighborhoods all over the United States. You can search for available properties, research loans and financing, investigate the cost of contracting work and repairs on fixer-upper properties, and calculate the total costs of purchasing a new or older home. You can even search for foreclosed properties, using the RealtyTrak.com engine.

■ **Yahoo! Real Estate** (*http://realestate.yahoo.com*) connects you to a wealth of information about finding, buying, financing, and closing on real estate. You get access to mortgage calculators, foreclosed property listings, and agents serving a particular geographic region, as well as in-depth articles about the current condition of the real estate market on a city-by-city basis.

■ **HomeGain** (*www.homegain.com*) can help you find a local agent, assess the value of a property, locate homes for sale, apply for a mortgage, and more. It includes links to sites that provide you with reports on local schools, as well as employers.

■ **Zillow** (*www.zillow.com*) provides useful data for buyers, including interactive maps that let you zoom in on the neighborhoods that interest you. Then it shows you the prices of recently sold homes so you can get a sense of neighborhood market trends. If you're interested in a particular property, you can enter its street address into an estimation engine and get an approximate range showing what the property is worth.

INSIDER'S INSIGHT

E-Pro Certification

"Always ask if your Realtor is E-Pro Certified. This is a certification program sponsored by the National Association of Realtors to make sure Realtors know everything there is to know about using the Internet to help their clients. It saves buyers an enormous amount of trouble to have an agent who can teach them how to use the Internet to their best advantage."

Cristy Shaw, Broker,
Keller Williams Realty,
Orange Beach, Alabama

Bargains— or Buyer Beware?

T he thought of getting a deal on a property can be very appealing. And bargain properties are out there: homes that have been foreclosed or that are in probate often sell for less than the going market rate. So do cheaper fixer-uppers that need what sellers euphemistically call "tender loving care."

Although there *are* deals, when it comes to home buying, there are no free lunches. If something seems too good to be true, it probably is. Houses that sell for less than the market rate usually come with complications: these can be financial (the property has been foreclosed), legal (the previous owner died without a will), logistical (long-term tenants occupy the premises), or physical (major repairs are needed). If you are considering a "bargain" home, understand the tradeoffs that may be involved.

Foreclosures

A foreclosure is a legal proceeding in which a bank or other creditor takes possession of a piece of real estate after the owner fails to make mortgage payments. The county sheriff or some other officer of the court then holds an auction to sell the property to the highest bidder. Because of the unusual circumstances surrounding the re-sale of the property, foreclosures have traditionally been viewed as a means of acquiring real estate at less-than-market prices.

Foreclosures are not happy events. The people whose mortgages were foreclosed might not have gone willingly. They might have taken fixtures, trashed the place, or made it difficult or even impossible for someone else to live there without spending thousands of dollars in repair or renovation work. Most financial institutions won't allow you to inspect a foreclosed property before bidding on it—and what you find after winning an auction might not be what you'd hoped for. Moreover, many foreclosures are tangled legal affairs with lots of potentially nasty surprises in them, such as the fact that there could be multiple claims to ownership of the property. Although there is the potential for significant payoff, your tolerance for risk is critical. It's also vital to hire a competent lawyer to advise you through the entire process.

Probate houses

A probate sale occurs when a homeowner dies and a property must be sold in order to pay debts or divide assets among multiple inheritors.

The idea behind successful probate home purchasing—and there are dozens of books, websites, and seminars dedicated to the subject—is that at any given time there are tens of thousands of estates in probate court. The executors of such estates, it is commonly assumed, want nothing more than to quickly settle up the affairs of the deceased and give the funds to the proper inheritors. The challenge in probate purchases is locating property that is currently in probate, finding the executors who have the power to sell that property, and convincing them to accept less than the property would fetch if auctioned off to the general public.

Each of these steps has its challenges. Moreover, there's the issue of financing: if you can't pay the seller when you make

Get Rich Quick?

There's now an entire industry dedicated to helping people find and buy foreclosed properties, based on the premise that they represent enormous bargains. Do an Internet search on "real estate" and "foreclosure" and you'll end up with millions of hits. Recognize that these aren't the actual foreclosures themselves, although there are ever-increasing numbers of websites that allow you to search for foreclosures in a particular zip code. Instead, these search results are for sites that want to sell you how-to guides on buying foreclosed properties, lists of foreclosed properties, lists of pre-foreclosed properties ... it goes on and on.

Foreclosed properties do tend to sell at auction for less than going market rates. But there are considerable risks involved. In particular, be wary of people who claim they can help you find and close on such properties for a fee. Although some of them are legitimate, many are advocates of dubious "get-rich-quick" schemes. Indeed, the number of real estate fraud investigations initiated by IRS Criminal Investigation (CI) doubled between 2001 and 2003. Make sure you aren't one of the victims.

the deal—and few first-time home buyers can—you'd have to convince the seller to work with you on that. And the more the process resembles a traditional home purchase, the less motivated the seller will be to discount the property.

Fixer-uppers and "contractor's specials"

These terms can mean anything from a property that needs a new roof to one with serious plumbing or electrical problems to one that needs to be rebuilt from the foundation up.

Buying a fixer-upper allows you to take possession of a home you wouldn't have been able to afford if it had been in perfect repair. Say you'd like to live in the neighborhood with the state's highest-ranking schools, but the properties there are priced out of your reach. Purchasing a home in the area that needs its electrical and plumbing redone and still has its original kitchen and bathrooms might be the only way you can afford property in that district.

Many fixer-uppers are not in "move-in condition." First-time buyers do move in, though—mostly because they can't afford to pay rent at the same time as paying a mortgage. A lot of energy, hard work, and time, and a fair bit of cash, are required to help a fixer-upper reach its full potential. So figure these into the cost of any purchase.

In a seller's market, fixer-uppers are often sold "as is." Buyers eager to break into the market accept things that they ordinarily wouldn't—like a leaking roof or an aging electrical system. In buyer's markets, it's usually much harder to find takers for fixer-uppers—and the prices are discounted, sometimes significantly.

Tenant-occupied houses

Tenant-occupied homes—or properties that are currently being rented out to people other than the owners—might seem to offer unique opportunities for first-time home buyers. But be aware that tenant-occupied properties are frequently not in as good shape as owner-occupied properties. A house that has seen a succession of renters over the years is often the worse for wear. There could also be complications with the tenants themselves when the deed changes hands. Some cities or counties—particularly those with strong rent-control laws or active tenants' rights organizations—have stringent requirements about what is allowed during relocation or eviction. Although change of ownership and moving into the house or unit yourself is a legal means of getting control of a property, some rent-control districts—Los Angeles, for example—require that the existing tenants be paid relocation fees that can add up to many thousands of dollars.

There is also the danger that the tenant will simply refuse to move out at the time the property legally changes hands. Although not common, this can result in significant legal fees and hassles when it does occur. If there are any signs of tension or hostility on the part of existing tenants toward the pending sale, consider consulting a lawyer before proceeding with an offer.

Where the Heart Is

"*Although there are many factors to buying a house, you also have to go with your heart. When you see the right house, it's something you feel, and can picture yourself in.*"

Gary Love, Realtor,
Realty South,
Birmingham, Alabama

View Properties

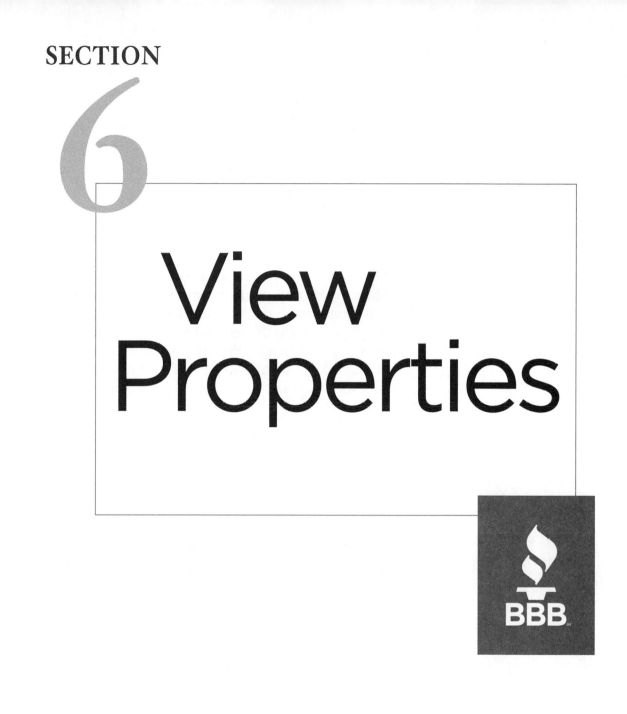

Start the Search

F or many home buyers, looking at houses is the most exciting part of the venture. The amount of information available on the Internet, combined with the increasing availability of agents offering their services "à la carte" (see page 35), means that growing numbers of home buyers are taking on a bigger chunk of the responsibility when it comes to purchasing even their first properties.

Nevertheless, 85 percent of first-time home buyers will use agents for some or all of the purchasing process. One of the primary reasons for this is that agents offer quick and easy *access* to properties. Although there's probably an MLS that covers your area, you might not be able to log onto it. You may need an agent just to be able to see what's listed. You could track down the listing agent for a particular property that you'd like to view, but this could be time consuming and frustrating. You frequently won't know until you call the agent how many bedrooms or baths a property has or what the asking price is.

Moreover, good agents stay on top of what is happening with properties in their area. They may have previous clients who are preparing to sell a house that isn't yet on the market. They're likely to go to weekly agents-only viewings of newly listed homes, giving their clients a head start on the open houses and saving them time by eliminating homes clearly not of interest.

In short: if you don't use an agent, you'll be out of the loop when it comes to viewing properties. And this will be a major disadvantage—especially to inexperienced, first-time buyers.

What to expect

Today, almost all real estate professionals start a house hunt with the computer. Typically, they sit with you in their office and search through the MLS (see page 78) to identify the properties that seem most relevant given the "needs" and "wants" list you have put together. Take a copy of the worksheet you completed on page 12 when you meet with your agent to go through the MLS.

You should also take the addresses of any properties you've spotted yourself that you're interested in viewing—such as one you've seen online or in a classified ad or because you saw a "for sale" sign on your dream street.

Be very specific about the way you would like to work. For example, you may want to come up with a shortlist of two or three properties before you ask your agent to schedule a visit. Or you may want to pile into the car—either yours or the agent's—and do a whirlwind trip around town, viewing as many as six or seven properties in one day.

In a buyer's market, there will be many more properties to view, and you can see them more or less at your convenience. You may spread your house-hunting expeditions out over days, even weeks. But in a fast-moving seller's market, you might be lucky to find two or three properties that fit your criteria and price range at any given time. Be ready to view properties as soon as they become available.

Prepare yourself for information overload! Take a pen and paper and make notes. Not only will you be given lots of factual information about properties, including square footage, lot size, and the age and condition of important features such as roofs, boilers, and heating or air conditioning units, but you will be bombarded with a great deal of *sensory* information. You'll have strong visceral reactions to properties as you see, touch, smell, and hear what it would be like to occupy the physical space.

If You Go Solo

People who choose to buy a home without the services of an agent usually do it to save money. It might not be obvious how that would happen—after all, the seller, not the buyer, pays the agents' fees. But think of it this way: the seller typically pays 6 percent of the sales price in commissions: 3 percent goes to the seller's agent and 3 percent to the buyer's agent. If you're going it alone, you could make the case that *you* should get the 3 percent that would have gone to the buyer's agent—that, in effect, 3 percent of the sales price should be knocked off the property. Depending on what you are paying, this can be tens of thousands of dollars. But there's no guarantee that you will actually be able to convince a seller to reduce the price on this basis. This approach may also narrow the choice of homes you can consider. And you'll have to do without the advice of an agent when dealing with the lengthy paperwork associated with the purchase.

Take the Tour

A fter you've selected a list of potential properties from the MLS, your agent will drive you to them. If a home is vacant, you can view it at any time. When a home is occupied, the agent is usually asked to call before showing up. After you arrive at the property, the agent will take a key from a lockbox on the door and go inside with you. Some properties—those with dangerous pets, messy children, or a family illness—can be seen by appointment only. Your agent will contact the seller and/or the listing agent to decide on a time that is convenient for all.

Once inside, gather as much information as you can as efficiently as you can. The information you collect should not be just factual. You should also pay attention to your *emotional* reaction to each property. How does the property make you feel? Are you comfortable in the neighborhood? In the home itself? Is it a place you can picture yourself living?

QUICK TIP

A Change of Heart

Once you begin to view properties, expect to modify the contents of your "wants" and "needs" lists—sometimes considerably. You'll discover things that will alter your vision of the perfect home. Perhaps you were convinced you wanted a condo because of the easy maintenance, but then found yourself put off by how close the neighbors would be. Or perhaps you hadn't rated a remodeled kitchen high but learned that you can't imagine living in a house with an outdated oven. Visiting properties helps you clarify your priorities.

Sellers—and their agents—are very conscious that a strong positive reaction to a property can make a sale. They do their best to "stage" or present a property to its best advantage in order to tempt prospective buyers (see below). Don't be so distracted by an elegant flower arrangement that you fail to notice the leaky roof. On the other hand, in houses that *haven't* been staged, you could be so put off by the shag carpeting and psychedelic wallpaper that you miss out on a place that would be absolutely perfect without these cosmetic defects. Sometimes you have to perform a delicate balancing act, weighing the cold, hard facts about a piece of property—its size, construction quality, general condition, and location—against its softer, less easily quantifiable, appeal.

Staging Strategies

Although the majority of properties for sale are still occupied by their owners, an increasing number are "staged," which is industry lingo for taking a home and decorating it with rented furniture, artwork, and other accessories to make it look as appealing as possible. The goal: to sell a property for a higher price than it would get if shown with the owner's possessions.

Tricks of the staging trade include using smaller-scale furniture—and much less of it—so that rooms appear bigger; painting walls a neutral color such as white or pale gray to freshen up a small space; installing new, light-colored carpeting to make rooms seem more open and bright; putting in sod and decorative plants to increase a property's "curb appeal"; or even baking fresh cookies to make a place smell like "home."

Don't let a new coat of paint charm you away from investigating meatier issues like a crack in the foundation or a damp spot on the ceiling. And when a home hasn't been staged, don't let the current owner's terrible taste or housekeeping habits prevent you from making an offer on a home with lovely bones and sturdy workmanship.

INSIDER'S INSIGHT

Love at First Sight

"It's difficult when a client falls in love with one of the first properties he or she sees. Because they haven't viewed a lot of options, they might not know what they really want. But if they pass it up, they might never feel the same way about another property. It's important to proceed very carefully in such cases. If there are no other offers pending on that particular home, they should definitely take their time to look around. But if it's a competitive market, they might want to step up and make their offer."

Lovinda Beal, Agent,
Cornish & Carey,
Portola Valley, California

Home-touring etiquette

Many first-time buyers aren't sure what to do when they're viewing properties. If the seller or tenant hasn't moved out yet, you might be reluctant to intrude on what, after all, is still someone's private residence.

Drop this attitude as soon as possible. You are making one of the biggest decisions of your life—so it's no time to be timid. Open closets and look in kitchen cabinets. Turn on the shower taps in the bathroom and flush the toilets. Venture into attics and basements. Just don't snoop in drawers, remove objects, or do anything to damage the property. Picking up rugs to look at the floor underneath is fine, as is moving objects—gently—in order to examine some aspect of a room more carefully. Just be sure you put everything back the way it was.

The first visit

The first time you visit a property, check to see that it fits your most basic needs. In subsequent visits, you'll dig deeper. Your first job is to eliminate properties that are obviously inappropriate.

You'll be able to tell right away if a property is *not* for you. Even if it looks perfect on paper and fits all the "needs" on the worksheet you filled out on page 12, pay attention if you have a strong negative response to it. Yes, there are properties that don't show well but could be fixed up to feel more attractive and welcoming (and which can offer you good value as a result). Your agent will advise you when that's the case. Still, your agent is not going to live there; you are. Purchasing a home is an emotional, as well as a financial, decision. Listen to your instincts.

Another indefinable attribute is *charm*. This one is also highly individualized and difficult to quantify. You know it when you see it. That utterly enchanting top-floor condominium might seem claustrophobic to your agent, who could point out that you might have trouble finding a buyer when you are ready to sell. You might be enamored of that vintage cottage with the overgrown garden, but all your agent can see are the repair and maintenance bills—and the backaches from the do-it-yourself projects that would be in store for you. Even if you've fallen in love with a property, it's a good idea to listen to a more level-headed assessment before proceeding. You may still choose to go with your instincts. But ask at least one person to play devil's advocate to help you test your decision.

QUICK TIP

When Once Must Be Enough

Sometimes you won't have the opportunity for a second visit. Usually this is because the market is so hot that it's likely there will be an offer (or even multiple ones) made by the time you get back with your tape measure. In such cases, you might have to just go ahead and make your offer.

The second visit

You'll begin your house hunt by paying quick visits to a number of properties and eliminating most of them. In general, you'll decide right away whether or not a particular property will stay on your "possibles" list. That's when the real work begins. First, you'll make a return visit to investigate the two to four properties you liked best.

Your second visit will last up to an hour and be much more systematic than the first. Instead of depending on your impressions, take along additional tools to help you make up your mind about the suitability of the property:

- **Camera or video recorder.** A picture is still worth a thousand words. Take your camera and photograph everything: the interiors of all the rooms, the exterior of the property (all four walls, whether it's a house or a condo; the roof; the foundation), and the yard if there is one. If you have a video camera, all the better. Take photos of any aspect of the house that seems dubious, such as an aging roof, sagging gutters, or a cracked foundation. If the market is slow enough to give you the time, you can show the pictures to contractors for estimates of what it might cost to repair and/or replace things. A visual record will also help you refresh your memory as you sift through the house's features when preparing to make an offer.

- ■ **Measuring tape.** Use this on anything that can be measured. Record the dimensions of all the rooms. If any of the doors seem smaller than standard size, measure those as well. You don't want your cherished credenza to get stuck in the front door!

Your pre-inspection

When you make an offer on a home, you should specify in the contract that if the property does not pass inspection, the offer will be canceled. Only in rare circumstances would a buyer make an offer without this condition. The inspection can range from one general house inspector going over the entire premises to an army of inspectors, each investigating a different aspect of the house. They will give you recommendations about any defects and work that needs to be done.

But it's still a good idea for you to do your own preliminary inspection. You may find some dealbreakers that will cause you to reject the property before you go any further. If you see evidence of problems but still want to proceed, your pre-inspection will save you time and effort later as you can take into account any obvious defects when putting together your offer. Look carefully at these things:

- ■ **Overall condition of the exterior.** Have the owners taken care of the property and kept major features, such as the roof, the grounds, and the gutters, well maintained and up to date? Is there evidence of standing water on the property? Are the gutters askew or cluttered with leaves? Is the chimney leaning over? How about the window frames: are they straight and unwarped?

■ **Overall condition of the interior.** Is it hot or cold compared to the external temperature? Are there any unpleasant smells? What is the condition of the flooring—the wood, the linoleum, or the carpeting? Will they need to be replaced or refinished? What kinds of heating and/or cooling systems does the house have? Are door frames straight? Do doors close completely? Are any cupboards hanging off their hinges?

■ **Plumbing.** Turn on the taps. What's the water pressure—on the sink taps as well as in the bathtubs and showers? What's the capacity of the boiler? Do the toilets flush readily?

■ **Electrical system.** Are there sufficient electrical outlets placed conveniently throughout the rooms? How old is the wiring?

■ **Pests and damp.** Look for any evidence of termites or vermin (check underneath sinks and in basements for dampness and/or animal droppings). Are there places where wood meets the raw ground (with no cement or stone or other barrier keeping termites from the house)? Are the basement and the garage dry? Is there any sign that the owners won't store things in either place?

■ **Utilities.** Is the house fueled by electric energy? Natural gas? Propane? Some combination? What are the average monthly utility bills? Is garbage collection included in this?

INSIDER'S INSIGHT

Condo Rules and Fees

If you're considering a condo, get the rules and guidelines [officially called Covenants, Conditions & Restrictions, or CC&Rs] immediately. It's very important that you understand all the restrictions on your use, decoration, and remodeling of the property, as well as what maintenance is covered by the association by the monthly fees. Roof repairs and street repairs are probably included, but make sure the association has enough cash in reserve to handle any large upcoming projects, such as painting the complex or overhauling the pool area. The last thing you want is an unpleasant surprise once you've closed.

Pat Perelli, Realtor and BBB member,
John Hall & Associates,
Phoenix, Arizona

Rate Properties

Rating properties is a very personal and subjective process. Much of how you rate a house has as much to do with your gut reaction as to your conclusions based on facts and physical features. Use the following worksheets to take notes about the properties you return to for second visits and to compare them to each other in a systematic way.

Although many characteristics about properties are difficult to quantify, you probably have some minimum *physical* requirements, such as the number of bedrooms or bathrooms or overall square footage. Use the worksheets to record your observations about these items. If you plan to visit more than three properties, copy the forms so you have additional space to record your findings.

Physical characteristics

Record physical characteristics of the homes that interest you most, including the square footage of each room; the existence of closets, windows, hardwood floors, and carpeting; and special features such as fireplaces, appliances, and other attributes.

	PROPERTY 1	PROPERTY 2	PROPERTY 3
Address			
Living room			
Dining room			
Kitchen			
Family room			
Den/office			

	PROPERTY 1	PROPERTY 2	PROPERTY 3
Bedroom 1			
Bedroom 2			
Bedroom 3			
Bedroom 4			
Basement			
Attic			

	PROPERTY 1	PROPERTY 2	PROPERTY 3
Bathroom 1			
Bathroom 2			
Bathroom 3			
Overall size of house			
Lot			
Other			

Property Rating

For each property you are seriously considering, fill in the bubbles to the right of each characteristic using a scale of 1 to 10, where 1 is the worst and 10 is the best. Make copies of this worksheet so you can fill one in for every home you are considering.

Once you've completed this worksheet for every property you're evaluating, you'll have a clear graphical representation of how each one compares on the attributes that are most important to you.

	1	2	3	4	5	6	7	8	9	10
Size	O	O	O	O	O	O	O	O	O	O
Charm	O	O	O	O	O	O	O	O	O	O
Age	O	O	O	O	O	O	O	O	O	O
Condition	O	O	O	O	O	O	O	O	O	O
Upkeep	O	O	O	O	O	O	O	O	O	O
Location	O	O	O	O	O	O	O	O	O	O
Yard	O	O	O	O	O	O	O	O	O	O
Parking	O	O	O	O	O	O	O	O	O	O
Kid-friendly	O	O	O	O	O	O	O	O	O	O
Pet-friendly	O	O	O	O	O	O	O	O	O	O
Price	O	O	O	O	O	O	O	O	O	O
Other	O	O	O	O	O	O	O	O	O	O
_____	O	O	O	O	O	O	O	O	O	O
_____	O	O	O	O	O	O	O	O	O	O
_____	O	O	O	O	O	O	O	O	O	O
_____	O	O	O	O	O	O	O	O	O	O
_____	O	O	O	O	O	O	O	O	O	O
_____	O	O	O	O	O	O	O	O	O	O
_____	O	O	O	O	O	O	O	O	O	O
_____	O	O	O	O	O	O	O	O	O	O
_____	O	O	O	O	O	O	O	O	O	O
_____	O	O	O	O	O	O	O	O	O	O
_____	O	O	O	O	O	O	O	O	O	O
_____	O	O	O	O	O	O	O	O	O	O

Property Rating

For each property you are seriously considering, fill in the bubbles to the right of each characteristic using a scale of 1 to 10, where 1 is the worst and 10 is the best. Make copies of this worksheet so you can fill one in for every home you are considering.

Once you've completed this worksheet for every property you're evaluating, you'll have a clear graphical representation of how each one compares on the attributes that are most important to you.

	1	2	3	4	5	6	7	8	9	10
Size	O	O	O	O	O	O	O	O	O	O
Charm	O	O	O	O	O	O	O	O	O	O
Age	O	O	O	O	O	O	O	O	O	O
Condition	O	O	O	O	O	O	O	O	O	O
Upkeep	O	O	O	O	O	O	O	O	O	O
Location	O	O	O	O	O	O	O	O	O	O
Yard	O	O	O	O	O	O	O	O	O	O
Parking	O	O	O	O	O	O	O	O	O	O
Kid-friendly	O	O	O	O	O	O	O	O	O	O
Pet-friendly	O	O	O	O	O	O	O	O	O	O
Price	O	O	O	O	O	O	O	O	O	O
Other	O	O	O	O	O	O	O	O	O	O
_____	O	O	O	O	O	O	O	O	O	O
_____	O	O	O	O	O	O	O	O	O	O
_____	O	O	O	O	O	O	O	O	O	O
_____	O	O	O	O	O	O	O	O	O	O
_____	O	O	O	O	O	O	O	O	O	O
_____	O	O	O	O	O	O	O	O	O	O
_____	O	O	O	O	O	O	O	O	O	O
_____	O	O	O	O	O	O	O	O	O	O
_____	O	O	O	O	O	O	O	O	O	O
_____	O	O	O	O	O	O	O	O	O	O
_____	O	O	O	O	O	O	O	O	O	O

Everything Is Negotiable

"Everything is negotiable with new homes. In slower markets in particular, builders can be anxious to move properties. I had a client who talked the builder down $59,000 just by being patient and going back to them every month."

Joe Loparo,
Realtor, Gallagher & Lindsay,
Alameda, California

Buying *a* New Home

Advantages of Buying New

N ew home construction has been booming. In 2005, 1.7 million single-family homes were built in the United States—the highest number recorded since the U.S. Census Bureau began tracking housing starts in 1959. Many first-time buyers prefer to buy a new home rather than an existing one because, well, it's *new*. They like the idea of walking over the threshold of something that is theirs from the very beginning.

Advantages of buying a new home

Just imagine: no one else's hideous carpet to tear up. No ugly wallpaper to rip off. No leaks in the roof or clanking in the pipes, and doors and windows that open and close easily. There are many advantages to buying new: A freshly built home offers:

- **Easier and cheaper maintenance.** You don't have to worry about worn carpets or scratched floors, loose tiles, or unreliable plumbing. Your life will be a lot easier—and your monthly budget for home upgrades and repairs both lower and more predictable.

- **Bigger dimensions.** New homes tend to feature more spacious rooms and higher ceilings than do older homes. There's also more likely to be an open floor plan, giving the home a more expansive feel.

INSIDER'S INSIGHT

Upgrades

"Keep in mind that it's not only price that is negotiable. Be aware of the types of upgrades that a builder is offering—such as granite countertops, Jacuzzi baths, more windows—and ask for them to be thrown in with the purchase price. Especially in slower markets, builders need to find ways to attract buyers, and including free upgrades is a very common way of doing this."

Noah Seidenberg,
Agent, Coldwell Banker,
Evanston, Illinois

- **More bathrooms.** New homes generally have a minimum of three and sometimes even four or five full baths. This adds to the livability and comfort of a house, especially for a growing family.

- **New appliances.** Newly built homes have modern appliances, giving you the advantages of the latest features and more years of use before replacement.

- **More storage space.** Closets are bigger and more plentiful in newer homes. Oversized walk-in closets are often standard in master bedrooms. Basements and garages are larger, too.

- **A home office.** With so many people starting their own businesses or working at home at least some of the time, a home office is becoming more common in many newer homes. Houses now often include a first-floor room that can be used as either a home office or an extra bedroom.

- **Possibility for customization.** Depending on the type of home you buy (see pages 110-111), you can specify precisely the features you want, from fireplaces to patios, porches to hardwood floors, kitchen counters to bathroom fixtures.

- **Energy efficiency.** New homes have better insulation and energy-efficient appliances. This is not only good for the environment; it also lowers your utility bills.

- **Technology readiness.** New houses are increasingly ready for advanced telecommunications services such as cable and high-speed Internet access.

- **Environmentally sound.** None of the environmental hazards of older homes are likely to be a problem: no asbestos, lead-based paints, formaldehyde, or other known toxic substances will be present when you move in.

- **Financing available.** Builders will frequently have relationships with lenders and can streamline the mortgage application process, making it easier to qualify for and secure adequate financing.

Warranty Included

Most new homes come with warranties that cover nearly all defects for the first year. Usually there is limited coverage for the following years (check the fine print to understand exactly what is covered and for how long). And you can frequently upgrade the warranty either by paying an additional fee to the builder or by purchasing a contract with an independent home warranty company.

INSIDER'S INSIGHT

Getting into a New Home

Builders are very friendly to first-time buyers. In our area, builders often have a 'grand plan' package for getting you into a home that includes financing, and covers the down payment and all closing costs, often for as little as $1,000 out of pocket. And don't forget, with a new home you know exactly what you are dealing with—you're not buying someone else's problems.

Cristy Shaw, Broker Associate,
Keller Williams Realty,
Orange Beach, Alabama

Construction Quality

A new home will only be as good as its builder. So do your research before you go near any development. Ask your real estate agent if they have heard of the builder and search for articles about the company, especially any with references to lawsuits or construction quality. Visit other developments the builder has completed—preferably ones that were built some years ago—and see how they've stood the test of time. Don't hesitate to knock on doors and ask how satisfied the residents are with the quality and the after-sales service provided. And, of course, check with your local Better Business Bureau to see if any complaints have been lodged against the builder.

Just because a home is new doesn't mean there won't be problems. If a new house you're considering has already been built, make sure you hire an inspector, just as you would if buying an existing home. It's well worth the money to have a competent inspector spot a poorly constructed foundation, low-quality flashing, or other defects. If the builder hasn't yet broken ground on your particular house, hire an inspector to look over the construction at key points in the building process (see page 117).

If you're very concerned about quality and want to reduce your risks even further, you can get a homeowner's warranty from an independent warranty company to cover everything from roofs to plumbing, air conditioning, and foundation problems.

QUICK TIP

The Early Buyer Gets the Discount

Builders frequently offer significant discounts, or free upgrades, to people buying into a development early. You're especially likely to save thousands off the price if you commit to purchasing a home before the ground has been broken. The longer you wait—especially if you delay until the houses are finished and filling up—the more you'll pay.

Disadvantages of Buying New

A lthough buying a new home offers many advantages, it also presents a number of potential pitfalls. Consider these disadvantages and weigh them against the attractions of purchasing new. First-time buyers should visit at least two or three existing properties as a matter of course to get a feel for the difference between living in a home of the latest construction versus a "preowned" one. Some of the disadvantages of purchasing new:

■ **Pricier.** On a square-foot basis, new homes are generally more expensive than existing ones. That's because new homes tend to have more generous dimensions and routinely possess what used to be considered luxurious amenities like central air conditioning, two- or three-car garages, and the latest appliances.

■ **Small (or nonexistent) yard.** Land is expensive, so builders in recent years have squeezed increasingly large houses onto increasingly small lots. If a new house *does* have a yard, it's likely not more than dirt. All the trouble—and expense—of putting in landscaping is yours.

QUICK TIP

Ghost Towns

Although you could get a discount—and sometimes a substantial one—for buying early in a development, there are a number of risks involved. One of them is that if homes sell very slowly, you may find yourself one of the few lonely inhabitants of a community. If you put off your purchase, you might pay a little more and you might have to wait longer to take possession of your house. But a later deal greatly reduces the risk of being surrounded by a sea of uninhabited—or even worse, half-finished—dwellings.

- **Inconvenient location.** Newer developments tend to be in out-of-the way places, relatively far away from city centers. You're likely to have longer commutes to work, schools, shopping, and entertainment.

- **Special fees and assessments.** Like condominiums and townhomes, many new communities have association fees and CC&Rs (Covenants, Conditions, and Restrictions) that govern what you can do with your property. If the development is very new, the city might also impose a special assessment on property owners in order to build traffic lights, sewers, or schools.

- **Settling problems.** Every new house has to "settle" into its site. How much depends on the soil, the other geological attributes of the location, and the materials of the house, as much as the quality of construction. Expect some settling as normal. But you might find significant cracks appearing in walls and around door-frames or discover that windows become difficult or even impossible to open and close. In most cases, severe settling will be covered by your homeowner's warranty. Make sure that's specified before you sign the contract.

- **Discrepancy between plans for landscaping and reality.** The sketches of that new park and playground, the tree-lined boulevards, and the lushly landscaped common areas look terrific on paper but might not live up to your expectations once they are completed. It's expensive to purchase and install mature plants and trees, so developers usually plant seedlings that will look unimpressive for some time to come.

- **Delays in concerns being addressed by builder.** A homeowner's warranty doesn't protect you from builders who drag their feet when you need them to address problems. The last thing you want is the inconvenience and cost of taking your builder to court. The best way to avoid this problem is to research the builder ahead of time. Before you buy, ask the builder to disclose whether there are any pending or completed lawsuits against the firm.

■ **Non-competitive financing.** Like car dealerships, home builders often have relationships with lenders and offer their own financing plans to qualified buyers. Although these packages might seem attractive, be sure to do the math on what are typically variable-rate loans. Add up the upfront costs (points and other loan application or processing fees) to sniff out any "padding" with junk fees and to verify that the initial interest rate, margin, adjustment period, maximum rate, and rate adjustment cap (see Chapter 9) are all competitive with the current mortgage market.

Get Ready to Wait

The most common problem with buying a house before it's completely finished is that it might not be ready when it's supposed to be. In fact, you should *plan* on delays. And they are not always the builder's fault. Although construction can be held up by inept scheduling or poor planning, some things are unavoidable, such as bad weather that prevents the pouring of cement. Don't give notice to your landlord on the assumption that the house will be ready on the precise date named in the contract.

In the worst-case scenario, your builder could run out of money—and you would then lose your deposit as well as your dream home. This doesn't happen very often, but it does happen. Research a builder before signing any contract to make sure the company is established and has a track record of completing projects on time.

Select Your Home

I f you've chosen to buy a newer home, you have a number of decisions to make. First, you must select between tract, semi-custom, and custom construction. Then there's the task of evaluating the neighborhood. Finally, just as with an existing home, you have to negotiate and finalize the contract.

Types of homes

- **Tract.** Most new homes are based on what are called "standard designs," or architectural plans that have been optimized to meet certain square footage/cost goals. Builders usually offer you a choice of a small number of designs when you buy into a particular community. Although you can—and, indeed, are encouraged to—purchase upgrades for flooring, countertops, appliances, and bathroom and kitchen fixtures, you can't change anything structural about a standard tract home without incurring significant expense.

- **Semi-custom.** This type of construction provides you with a wider range of options to make your house your own. You're still choosing features from a "menu," but you can add decks and porches; change the number, location, or size of windows; or modify garage orientation or size. As you would expect, a semi-custom home costs more than a tract home.

- **Custom.** With a custom home, anything goes. A builder or architect helps you design everything from the

Misleading Models

Older homes are often "staged" to make them appear more attractive, and builders use many of the same design tricks to make their model homes seem warm and inviting. For instance, model homes almost always exhibit the highest-quality materials and all the upgrades possible. What you'll get will likely be quite different unless you are willing to pay for all the accoutrements. Always ask the salesperson exactly what is, and isn't, included in the basic home. The granite countertops and whirlpool bath you sighed over in the model are not necessarily standard features. If possible, arrange for a walkthrough of an actual home that is complete (or near completion) to see the unvarnished truth.

overall architectural style to the layout of the rooms, the type of the fixtures, and the exact tint of the paint. You can be as particular as you want, specifying details down to the manufacturer of the knobs on the cabinet doors. This is a very expensive route to take, and it is usually beyond the means of the first-time home buyer.

Use Your Agent

Any agent will be willing to represent you in buying a new house. But whether they are able to do this depends on the builder. Some builders don't include agents' fees in their price structures; you either buy directly from them or through a real estate agent who has been hired to represent the builder. Keep in mind that in such cases this person is the seller's agent—not yours. So you'll have to do all the heavy work of negotiating on your own.

In slower markets, builders tend to be much more flexible and will frequently agree to pay your agent their standard fee for the sale. This is the best of all possible situations, as your agent will then be able to give you support as you negotiate the price, verify the terms of the contract, and oversee the construction and closing of the deal.

Be wary if you go to visit model homes in new developments without your agent. If you "sign in" at the development—the office will almost always ask you to do so—you are legally establishing that the builder brought you in, not your agent. This may release the builder from paying a fee to your agent should you decide to buy.

Judge the Builder, Not the Home

No matter how attractive a particular house in a particular development looks, always research the builder before buying. Keep in mind that the quality of the construction and the builder's responsiveness to any issues that arise after the sale can be judged only on the builder's history with previous developments and home buyers. A snazzy design and the impressive floor plan of a model home won't tell you what the builder is really like.

Assess the development

Just as you would when purchasing an existing house, you must carefully assess the neighborhood of a new development. This can be challenging, since most things you are investigating are planned or projected, but they won't actually exist yet. Still, there are some specific points you can ask about before signing the contract:

- **The local school district.** First, make sure there *are* plans for schools. If you already have school-age children, you may have to resign yourself to a long commute when you first move into a new development. But request a meeting with the school superintendent and attend local school board meetings to get acquainted with the characteristics, standards, quality, and long-term goals of the district. Ascertain the district's commitment to serving the needs of your development.

- **Ratio of houses/lots sold to unsold.** The fewer lots or houses that have been sold, the more risks you face. You won't know whether there will be young families or retirees on your block, and you won't be able to predict whether the neighborhood will come together to form a cohesive community. On the other hand, you might welcome the opportunity to be a pioneer and take the lead in forming the character of a neighborhood.

QUICK TIP

Go Shopping

One of the potential drawbacks of living in a new community is that the commercial infrastructure—including grocery stores, drugstores, gas stations, banks, and other types of merchants and service providers—might not yet be in place. Investigate the location of the nearest shopping center and do a test run to see how long it takes you to get there. Ask the builder—and verify with the city planning department—what commercial development is planned and when it will be completed.

- **Plans for community landscaping**. It takes imagination to move beyond the piles of lumber and brick surrounding the half-constructed houses to visualize a neighborhood alive with trees, plants, and flowers. But if communal landscaping is important to you, make sure the builder specifies plans for this in your contract. If there is any ambiguity about what the builder has committed to do for the neighborhood, make sure it is resolved by your agent or lawyer before signing.

- **Public transit.** Look into the availability of mass transit services such as commuter trains, buses, shuttles, and trolleys. These are especially important in outlying developments, where commutes on crowded highways can stretch to several hours. Public transit services can make the difference between whether living in a new community is viable or not.

Commutes in New Communities

Since most new communities are built in outlying areas, commutes to school and work will likely be long. But there is another complication. Because of the volume of new developments being built on the outskirts of urban centers, the supporting highway infrastructure has frequently not kept pace with all the construction activity. This means that the local roads leading into a city center or feeding into the regional highway system frequently cannot bear the increased traffic. And the highways themselves are often overwhelmed by the larger volume of vehicles. This can result in virtual parking lots of idling cars filled with commuters trying to get to the same place at the same time. Rush hour can quickly become intolerably long—not to mention expensive.

Assess the Development/Neighborhood

Make copies of this worksheet and fill them out as you visit various developments, so you can review and compare them at your leisure. Keep in mind that although developers (and their sales representatives) will try to rush you into making an immediate decision, you probably have plenty of time to consider all your options. Make sure to take it.

FEATURE	DESCRIPTION	NOTES
Existing school? How far away? New school?		
Houses/lots sold vs. unsold		
Plans for building local commercial/ public amenities`		
Plans for landscaping		
Public transit		
Commute time to work		
Other		

The Building Contract

B uilders provide their own purchase contracts for new homes. They're very different from the contracts you would sign if you were purchasing an existing home, and they're full of terms that favor the builder. As with any legally binding document you sign, examine your contract carefully. If you have an agent helping you with the home purchase, enlist their help in examining every clause. If the builder did not allow you to use your own agent, hire a real estate lawyer to read the contract and advise you on any terms or conditions that must be modified or eliminated before you sign. Be on the alert for:

- **No completion date.** Nothing would please most builders more than to have you sign an open-ended contract that did not specify when they had to complete your home. Make sure that your contract is very clear about the date when your home will be ready. If possible, insert a clause into the contract that binds the builder to paying a financial penalty for missing the promised completion date.

- **Right to change elements of the house without notification.** Some builders slip in a clause that allows them to substitute materials, modify dimensions, or otherwise alter the design of the house under construction without telling you. Delete such language from the contract and substitute a clear requirement to notify you—and obtain your *written* approval—for any revisions to the original design specifications of the house.

■ **Right to move you to a different lot without notification.** This is a notorious trick of less scrupulous builders. Make sure the contract specifies the lot you have purchased for your home and that no changes may be made without your written approval.

■ **Unreasonable "change order" charges.** Although you should establish the particular features and specifications of your new home before you sign the contract, sometimes after-the-fact changes are necessary. In such cases, you shouldn't have to pay exorbitant charges on top of the actual costs incurred to make the change. Check the contract to make sure that "change order" charges are reasonable.

■ **No financing contingencies.** Virtually all conventional contracts for buying an existing home have a financing contingency that releases you from the contract if you should fail to obtain a mortgage. Your builder's contract should contain the same provision.

■ **Clauses restricting you to arbitration in case of disputes.** Should anything go wrong with your new home-buying experience, you need to retain the right to take the builder to court. But many builders include language in their contracts that force you to use binding arbitration in case of disputes. This prevents you from suing them for redress of perceived wrongs. If such language exists, remove it.

Quick Tip

Hire a Contractor

Items to inspect at each stage of construction vary. Most, if not all, involve the "infrastructure" of the home that will be invisible once construction is finished. So much of what needs to be examined will be beyond the expertise of most first-time home buyers. That's why it's worth it to pay the $150 to $200 per visit that professional contractors will charge for their input. Even if they find one defect, your dollars will have been well spent, as this will save you enormous headaches—and money—further down the road.

Do the inspection

Once the contract has been signed, you might think you can sit back and wait for your new house to be completed. Not so. Inspecting your new home is just as important as inspecting a pre-owned one. No matter what the developer/builder assures you, you should make sure to take preliminary walkthroughs at critical points in construction and create a punch list that must be completed before closing.

Preliminary walkthroughs

Although you won't do the official walkthrough until construction is complete, it's a good idea to view the house at key points during its construction to inspect for shoddy workmanship or other things that can be fixed easily sooner rather than later. Better yet: hire a professional inspector to do walkthroughs with you. It's well worth spending the money to avoid potential headaches later on. Walk through the house:

- After the foundation has been poured

- After the framing is up

- After the house is wired and the plumbing is installed

- Before the walls are closed in

Punch lists

When you do your final walkthrough after the house is finished, be aware that it's not truly your last one. The "final final" walkthrough comes after the finishing touches—the items on your "punch list"—are finally completed. Only at this point can both you and the builder agree that construction is complete.

In the "first final" walkthrough, you'll examine every aspect of the house and make a detailed list of what still needs to be done. Leave nothing out! Is an electrical outlet missing a cover? Is the paint job in the living room shoddy? Is there a gap between the sink and the countertop? Did the workers leave debris in the yard? Don't assume that these small things will be taken care of automatically.

Once your punch list has been satisfactorily completed, you'll proceed with closing (see page 162). Closing on a new home is very much like closing on an existing one, although there are some minor differences, especially if you have arranged for financing from the builder.

Your Punch List

As you walk through the property, take detailed notes on everything you see that isn't to your complete satisfaction. Show this list to your builder. They may want to make a copy of it or they may have a form for you to fill out containing the same information. Keep referring to this list as the builder continues to work on your home. And do not sign the final papers at closing until *all* the items on the list have been addressed.

ITEM TO BE COMPLETED	NOTES	DATE COMPLETED

ITEM TO BE COMPLETED	NOTES	DATE COMPLETED

Keep Your Own Counsel

 Buyers should be very careful to keep their thoughts to themselves during the negotiation process. Make up your mind what you are willing—and able—to offer, and remain strong. Don't let emotions take over, or be biased by what anyone else is saying to pressure you to change your mind.

Noah Seidenberg, Agent,
Coldwell Banker,
Evanston, Illinois

Make *an* Offer

Calculate What You're Willing to Pay

O nce you've found a property you like, it's time to get down to the nitty gritty. You'll put in an offer and negotiate with the seller until you arrive at a price, and terms, that you both can agree to. The three steps you'll take before signing a contract:

- **Calculate what you're willing to pay.** The property you wish to purchase already has a price tag on it. This is called the *asking price*, and it's very far from being written in stone. In seller's markets, properties may go for tens of thousands of dollars above the asking price; in buyer's markets you may be able to get away with offering significantly less. Before you can decide what price to offer the seller, you need to determine, as best you can, the current *value* of the property given market conditions. Calculate this using hard numbers based on recent sales in the close vicinity. You will also need to

QUICK TIP

Discounting the Price

According to the National Association of Realtors (NAR), buyers, on average, offer 5 percent less than the asking price.

consider "softer" factors such as the general aesthetics and look and feel of the property in question.

Of course, your own emotions will also come into play. How badly do you want the home? You might be willing to pay a premium price because you've fallen in love with it. And there's the market itself to consider. In a seller's market, a property might receive multiple offers that boost the price sky high—perhaps beyond your reach. In a slower market, you may be able to pay less than asking price.

- ■ **Make an offer.** Once you've established how much you're willing to pay for your property, set down your offer in a formal document. Your offer will consist of much more than a dollar amount. It will also include the *terms* you desire, such as when you want to take possession of the property, how much money you'll give the seller up front, and any contingencies, or conditions, related to the sale.

- ■ **Negotiate with the seller.** After you make your first offer, the seller is likely to come back with a counteroffer. In this counteroffer, they will propose changes to the price and terms of your offer. You may go back and forth with the seller several times before arriving at a price and terms agreeable to both of you.

Asking versus selling price

How firm is the asking price? This depends on a multitude of factors, from the traditions of a local market to whether it's a buyer's or seller's market to the quirks of the listing agent to the seller's notion of what the property is worth.

Some properties will be priced very close to what the market justifies. Others will be priced significantly over that based on the assumption that buyers will make offers below the asking price. Sometimes a property is simply badly priced because the seller believes it's worth more than it actually is. That's why it's important to do your own independent calculations.

In most geographical areas it's assumed that a buyer will offer less than the asking price—usually 5 percent less—in a buyer's market. So you might try for even lower than that—although "lowballing" can have negative repercussions (see below). In a seller's market, all bets are off. If you find yourself in a multiple offer situation, you might submit an offer *over* the asking price.

QUICK TIP

The Lowball Offer

You might think you have nothing to lose by putting in a bid far below the asking price, but this is not necessarily true. A lowball offer can sour your chances of having any of your bids accepted or having a counteroffer made. That's because sellers are emotionally attached to their homes, and if they think you don't value it as you should or don't respect them enough to offer a decent price, they'll refuse to consider your offer and may turn deaf ears even if you want to try again with a more reasonable bid.

What You'll Pay for Premium Features

The precise premium that home improvements command varies from market to market. Every year, *Remodeling Magazine* (**www.remodeling.hw.net**), in conjunction with the National Association of Realtors, estimates the approximate national average increase in house price for various improvements. The following are results from the 2005 report.

FEATURE	APPROXIMATE PRICE PREMIUM FOR HOUSE
Remodeled kitchen	$15,000
Deck addition	$10,000
Basement refinished	$45,000
Remodeled bathroom	$10,000
Additional bathroom	$20,000
Replace windows with wood frame, double-glazed windows	$8,000
New roof	$9,000
Family room	$45,000
Additional master bedroom suite (additional bedroom plus bathroom)	$65,000

Comparative market analysis (CMA)

Now it's time to do a full-blown comparative market analysis (CMA) on the property you hope to own.

Your agent will use publicly available records to find out what properties in the neighborhood have sold recently—and for what price. Typically, an agent will try to find three to six properties that have sold within the last three or four months. If it's been a slow market, they might go back six to twelve months to find sufficient data. Your agent will then calculate the price per square foot of properties in that area and apply that factor to the one you've chosen. Other elements are then considered, such as the number of bedrooms and bathrooms, and upgrades or additional features such as a newly remodeled kitchen, a refinished basement, or a pool.

All this results in an approximate value of the property in question based on the current market. This price is usually expressed in a range, such as $250,000 to $265,000. If the seller is being realistic, the asking price shouldn't be far above this range, unless they have very tangible reasons for believing their property has some premium features that the CMA doesn't take into account. And this range gives you, the buyer, a good yardstick to use when deciding the offer to make on the property.

Keep in mind that a CMA is just an approximation. Each property is unique, and prices are driven by supply and demand. A property that is particularly charming—perhaps located on a private lot surrounded by mature trees—will carry a price premium. Your bank will also hire an inspector who will do a CMA to make sure you won't be paying more for the property than the market currently supports. Your application for a mortgage could be rejected if your offer exceeds that figure, so performing due diligence is very important.

Although traditionally buyers depended on their agents to "run the numbers," today you can go to a variety of websites,

Is Time on Your Side?

A property that's been on the market for a long time offers both a challenge and an opportunity. On the one hand, there could be something seriously wrong with the property, like a cracked foundation, a persistent drainage issue, or toxic wastes nearby. Have your agent ask around, and make sure to put strong inspection conditions in the offer before submitting it.

On the other hand, the seller could just have had some bad luck. Perhaps a previous sale collapsed at the last minute due to no fault of the seller. Or the seller initially held out for an unreasonable selling price and scared would-be buyers away. Sellers can be very motivated if their property hasn't sold as quickly as comparable ones on the market, and may be open to a lower price.

including Zillow.com (*www.zillow.com*), and see for yourself what has sold in the vicinity of a particular address, and for how much. By asking colleagues, an agent can usually ascertain why one property that on the surface looked very much like another sold for $20,000 more.

Property disclosures

When calculating the price you will offer, you also need to consider the cost of the repairs, remodeling, and reconditioning that will have to be done before the house is in move-in condition. In most states, sellers are required to disclose a host of things about a property before a contract is signed—sometimes on an official *disclosure form*. The seller must reveal "material facts" such as the age and condition of major components of the home, including the roof, water heater, heater and air conditioner, and any large appliances. Any structural defects must also be disclosed, as must lawsuits or other legal problems.

Use these disclosures to calculate how much it will cost to bring the house up to an acceptable level. Those calculations, in turn, will help you determine what to offer for a house. If the asking price is $350,000 and you determine that it will cost $12,000 to put on a new roof, it's reasonable to lower the price you are willing to pay or to ask the seller to take care of the repair before closing.

These disclosures don't replace the *inspection contingency* you'll put in your offer. A contingency is any condition that must be satisfied before the sale can be finalized. One of the most important contingencies will require that the property pass inspection by a professional, who will carefully examine all the critical components of the house from the foundation to the roof, including the electrical system and plumbing and including checking for termites. If the inspector finds anything wrong, the contingency gives you an out: you have the option of negotiating the contract further or walking away from it.

Comparative Market Anaysis

Your agent will probably provide you with a printout that looks like the worksheet below. But you may want to fill out the form yourself for your own records. Once you have your CMA, you should have a good sense of how the market values the property you want to purchase. This worksheet will thus make a critical contribution to how much you decide to offer on the house. You may even want to submit a copy of it when you provide the seller with your bid.

	THE PROPERTY YOU WANT TO BUY	COMPARISON PROPERTY 1	COMPARISON PROPERTY 2	COMPARISON PROPERTY 3	COMPARISON PROPERTY 4
Asking					
Sold					
Lot Size					
Bedrooms					
Bathrooms					
Total Square Feet					
Age					
Special Features					
Cost per Square Foot					

QUICK TIP

Call an Expert

Call contractors to get a realistic idea of the cost of fixing defects or of replacing important components before making your offer. They will have a better sense than either the seller or your agent about the actual costs of making repairs or improvements.

INSIDER'S INSIGHT

Inspection Advice

Traditionally, home inspections are performed after an offer has been accepted. But this is really backwards. I always recommend that people do an inspection before they make an offer. That way, they know exactly what they are getting into.

Joe Loparo, Realtor,
Gallagher & Lindsey,
Alameda, California

Putting it all together

You and your agent will consider a variety of factors—the asking price, the results of a CMA, the condition of the property, the estimated cost of repairs, and the type of market you are facing—to come up with the price you'll offer.

The price you offer and the price you are willing to pay for the property may be one and the same. But you may also choose to underbid slightly based on the assumption that the seller will come back with a counteroffer that increases the price. Most agents recommend the second approach in order to reserve negotiating room for later.

If you are not putting all your cards on the table and are willing to pay more than your first offer for the property, do *not* let anyone know what your maximum price is. This is especially true for your agent. Why? Agents are human and they get paid only if the sale goes through. They could be tempted to advise you to increase your price too quickly or succumb to pressure from the seller if they know your exact ceiling figure. When you refuse to reveal just how high you are willing to go, your agent will likely work harder on your behalf for a lower price.

Quick Tip

Disclosure Details

Even though your seller has filled out a disclosure form—usually the one provided by the state—it might not answer all your questions about a house. Ask the seller anything and everything you can think of—and get the answers in writing. When creating the offer, include as a contingency that everything the seller has told you will be verified by a professional inspection.

Make the Offer

An offer (officially called an *offer to purchase*) isn't just about price. Certainly, price is a big part of it. Sellers want to get as much as they can for a property, while one of your objectives is to minimize your outlay. But there are many other factors to consider. These are generally grouped under the heading *terms*.

Terms are such a critical part of the final contract that if multiple offers are made on a property—which can easily happen in a hot market—and two offers are comparable in price, terms will settle the matter. You can sometimes even offer *less* than others because your terms are so much more favorable from the seller's perspective. On the other hand, the more strict or rigid you are in demanding certain terms, the more likely the seller will reject your offer outright.

Anatomy of an offer

Your agent will probably use a standard form to prepare the offer. As with any contractual document, it will contain a number of standard elements. They include:

- Date that you make the offer

- Identification of buyer and seller, including legal names and current addresses

- Legal description of property, including the address, and such things as the parcel or lot number or other description as found in the deed.

INSIDER'S INSIGHT

Terms of Sale

"*I always recommend, instead of negotiating price, which a lot of sellers don't like doing, [to] negotiate for better terms. You can get them to throw in amenities—a refrigerator, or a new washer and dryer, or patio furniture. Sometimes you can get them to pay points and buy down the interest rate for you. You'd be surprised how much flexibility you have when negotiating terms rather than just price.*"

Cristy Shaw, Broker Associate, Keller Williams Realty, Orange Beach, Alabama

- The price you are offering

- Terms, including contingencies, concessions, and prorations

- Time and place of closing. Your agent will help you fill this out.

- Amount of earnest money (the money you will give to the seller upon the signing of the contract)

- Places for the signatures of both the buyer and the seller

QUICK TIP

Be Specific about Your Financing Needs

Make sure you are very specific about the terms of the financing you wish to secure. If you need a $150,000 mortgage but don't want to pay more than 6 percent interest with payments equal to or less than $750 month, specify this in your offer. If you don't include a statement about financing, you could possibly end up in the position of being contractually obliged to buy a house that you can't afford because financing didn't come through—or came through with an interest rate that would result in monthly payments you couldn't possibly meet.

Contingencies

The most important terms in a contract are called *contingencies*. These are the conditions that need to be met before the transaction can be completed. The two main contingencies are *financing* and *inspection*:

- **Financing contingency.** This is a standard component of most offers. In it you specify that your offer is dependent upon your securing appropriate financing. You should already be preapproved for a loan. Then, if the offer is accepted, you will apply officially for the funds and obtain final approval. The offer will usually specify a deadline by which financing must be secured. If the financing does not come through on time, the offer will be withdrawn.

■ **Inspection contingency.** If a defect has been disclosed by the seller or something is obviously defective about the property, you can specify in the offer that the seller must fix it before the sale is final. This is called a *concession* (see below). A concession can be anything from repairing a rotting deck to putting on a new roof. Many times you won't know everything about a property until you hire a professional inspector to look it over. To protect yourself against unpleasant surprises, put in a condition that the offer is contingent upon no serious problems being detected during the inspection.

The opposite of putting in an inspection contingency is to agree to accept the home "as is," no questions asked. You might do this in an extremely competitive market where you know there will be multiple offers on a property and you have no other way to distinguish your offer from others. (However, you would have to be willing to accept any defects that might be revealed during a later inspection.) "As is" offers are very attractive to sellers, as they know the sale will proceed without messy or expensive repair work or lingering concerns based on inspection reports.

Other aspects of the offer

An offer must also contain a number of other components:

■ **Concessions.** If you want the window treatments (which can be very expensive to replace) or appliances such as washers and dryers, stoves and refrigerators to be included in the sale, specify that in your offer. Feel free to ask for other things that appear to have been designed for the property and that would be difficult to move or fit into another home, such as custom bookcases or storage cabinets. Sellers will often agree to leave them behind.

You can also ask the seller to agree to financial concessions, such as paying for part of the cost of points or

Loss before Closing

If your contract, dated November 30, says that you will close on January 1, but on December 15 a major earthquake destroys the property, are you still required to go through with the contract? If the contract has not specified otherwise, you may have to. That's because common law says that if a piece of property is destroyed between the time a contract is signed and the time the deed is transferred—and if that destruction is not the fault of either the buyer or the seller—then the risk of loss belongs to the buyer. Although many states, including New York, have passed legislation that squarely puts the risk of loss onto the seller until the transaction is complete, it is best to make sure language specifying this is in the offer.

other fees associated with financing. Alternatively, you can ask the seller to pay for title insurance, property surveying, or some or all of the inspections.

What you can get depends on whether you are facing a buyer's or a seller's market. If a seller is extremely "motivated" (real estate jargon for desperate to sell), you can walk away with some key concessions.

Quick Tip

Meeting Your Match

Some people go through the entire buying process without ever seeing (or talking to) the seller. Either their agent handles all communication or the seller allows *their* agent to be the intermediary. Other sellers, however, are intimately involved. They want to meet all the prospective buyers, learn everything they can about them, and be at the negotiating table when offers are discussed. What your experience will be depends entirely on what you, the seller, and your respective agents (if you are using agents) are comfortable with.

- **Amount of earnest money.** This is the money you will give the seller upon signing the contract. Earnest money is not to be confused with the down payment that you give to the lender in order to secure your mortgage. The earnest money shows that you are serious about your offer. If the offer is accepted but you fail to go through with the contract for any reason other than those specified by contingencies, the seller keeps the earnest money. The earnest money can vary from 1 to 5 percent or even, in rare cases, 15 percent of the asking price of the property. The more competitive the market, the more earnest money you will be required to put down.

- **State of the property upon closing.** Don't assume that items such as light fixtures, porch swings, or garage storage cupboards are included in the sale. Neither should you take for granted that the junk in the garage and backyard will be taken away. Be very clear about the exact state that the property must be in when you take possession. Put language in the contract specifying that the property will be in the same general condition as it was when you signed the contract—that is, no new scratches on the floors, broken windows, or failed furnaces.

- **Prorations.** The offer should also contain explicit instructions about the way property taxes, utilities, homeowner's fees, and other payments that are either prepaid or paid in arrears will be divided (prorated) between buyer and seller. Say that a property was sold in September, but the annual property taxes came due in October. It wouldn't be fair for the buyer to pay taxes for the entire year, so the amount is prorated to make sure the seller pays their share.

- **Date of closing.** Specifying the date by which you want to take possession is an important aspect of the offer. Be aware that some sellers may want a short closing period, while others will want a longer one. Being sensitive to the needs of the buyer can go a long way toward getting you your home.

- **Deadline for responding to the offer.** No offer should be open ended. Specify a deadline by which the seller must either accept or reject it or submit a counteroffer. If that deadline passes, your offer will be withdrawn.

QUICK TIP

The Day Before

Be sure your offer specifies that you require a walkthrough 24 hours *prior* to closing. This will ensure that the seller has met all their legal responsibilities. It's better to find out that the sellers have substituted an old stove for the new one that was specified in the contract, or that they didn't put up drywall and repaint after some electrical work was done, *before* the home is legally yours—and while you therefore still have some leverage.

Terms of Your Offer

Fill in the following worksheet and use it to put together your formal offer.

COMPONENT	WHAT YOU PROPOSE
The proposed selling price (your offer)	
Any concessions you want the seller to make	
Financing contingencies	
Home inspection contingencies	
State of the property at the time of closing	
The amount of earnest money (your deposit)	
Prorations	
Time limit for responding to the offer	

Present the offer

You or your agent should *always* present the offer in person to the seller or the seller's agent. This usually involves a simple phone call to tell the seller and/or their agent that you're coming over with the offer. Sometimes, presenting the offer may be a more formal affair, particularly if there are multiple bidders for a property and the seller prefers to have everyone in the room at the same time. Why should you present the offer in person? No matter how thorough, the offer itself is a dry legal document. By putting a human face on it and giving it context, you will increase its chances of being accepted.

If you are offering less than the asking price, provide an explanation of how you calculated the figure, including a copy of your CMA and your estimate of needed repairs. In competitive markets where there are likely to be multiple bids, compose a personal letter to the seller, explaining your reasons for choosing that property. Under no circumstances should you criticize the property. And your agent should not fax an offer in except in very unusual circumstances.

Write a Letter

In a hot seller's market, when three, four, or even more people vie for the same property, you must distinguish yourself in any way you can. One way to do this is to write a letter to the seller, introducing yourself and providing convincing evidence that you're the right buyer for their home. Include:

◾ **Personal information.** Make the letter friendly and warm. Explain who you are, talk about your occupation and your interests. Introduce your spouse or partner and any other members of your family who will be living in the home. Provide a compelling portrait of yourself that will help the seller view you as a human being.

◾ **Praise for the property.** Emphasize what you like about the property and why it suits you so well. Talk about the look and feel of the place more than the quantitative aspects. For instance, you might mention that you're attracted to the house not just because it has three bedrooms, but because those three bedrooms are sunny and bright. If you're a gardener or if you appreciate the outdoors, comment on the landscaping. Praise the location or neighborhood.

◾ **Plans for the property.** Let the seller know some of the plans you have for the property as long as you're not aiming to do extensive remodeling or to scrap the house and build anew. If you intend to do some basic cosmetic repair and maintenance work without completely changing the character of the home, mention this. If there's a garden, it could comfort the seller to know you'll be giving it some loving attention. They'll look more favorably on your offer if they know you intend to take good care of the home they're leaving behind.

CHAPTER

25

Negotiate

Surviving the Pressure Cooker

One of the most time-honored tricks in the negotiating book is to have a seller (or seller's agent) tell you that other offers are pending and that you'll have to act fast and pony up additional money or concessions if you want the property. It's hard to resist these kinds of tactics. But keep a level head and determine what you are and aren't willing to pay. Establishing a baseline in a logical way will help you immeasurably during the heat of bargaining.

Once you've submitted your offer, the seller, or the seller's agent, will come back with one of three responses:

■ **Accept.** You're on your way to owning your dream home! Next you'll begin the inspection process and open escrow.

■ **Reject.** Perhaps there were multiple offers. Or you may have submitted an offer that was far too low or that had terms the seller couldn't accept. If the latter is the case, it's possible to try again. But keep in mind that your offer was probably well off the mark; otherwise, the seller would have responded with a counteroffer. If you want to give it another try, you'll have to rethink your strategy—and overcome some of the prejudice arising from your first offer.

■ **Counteroffer.** Although you might be disappointed that your offer wasn't accepted outright, this is actually good news. It means that you are close enough to the seller's terms that they want to negotiate.

A counteroffer will generally set out a compromise price that is lower than the asking price, but not as low as what you originally offered. And it may have changes—sometimes quite substantial—to the terms you offered. Perhaps the seller needs a 30-, rather than a 90-day, closing period. Or they may want to take all the appliances with them. Or they may want to stay in the house for a month after closing in exchange for paying rent. All these things are negotiable.

You can accept the counteroffer or decide to proceed with further negotiations. This process can go on for some time before you and the seller agree on terms.

Backup Offers

Sometimes you'll get a response to an offer that isn't simply accept, reject, or counteroffer. Sometimes a seller might tell you that your offer has been accepted as a "backup offer."

A backup offer is exactly what it sounds like. Someone else has submitted a winning bid, but you'll be next in line if that one falls through. In formally accepting your offer as a backup, the seller legally commits to signing a contract with you if the first offer fails for any reason. In highly competitive situations, more than one backup offer might be accepted. In such cases, the seller establishes a queue that specifies who is first, second, and third in line to get the property.

In the right circumstances, a little patience might actually win you your dream home. But you might also spend too much time waiting and hoping—when you could be looking around for other properties. One of the key things to do if you agree to have your offer as a backup is to make sure there's a clause that releases you from the contract should you find something else you'd like to buy. Otherwise, you could get stuck waiting for weeks or even months before you are free to continue your search.

Negotiating style

Whole books (and expensive courses) have been devoted to teaching successful negotiation skills. Some people believe that negotiations are win-lose propositions and persist in playing hardball, acting out good cop–bad cop scenarios, or attempting to bluff their way through. Others believe in compromise and in achieving win-win conclusions to negotiations. You—and your agent—will have to agree on the strategy you feel comfortable with.

There are a number of sound reasons to have the seller walk away from the negotiation table feeling satisfied, rather than defeated:

■ **They'll be motivated to turn the property over in tip-top condition.** The last thing you want is a disgruntled seller leaving a mess behind or, worse, reneging on contracted agreements to include window treatments, lighting fixtures, appliances, or other equipment or furniture along with the property. Sure, you'll be legally in the right to demand that such things be given to you, but do you really want to go through the headache and expense of a lawsuit? It's much better not to create any ill will to begin with.

■ **They'll cut you slack if and when you need it.** Although you might think you are on top of the home-buying process, problems always come up. You might need another month to find enough cash for the closing. Or you might have a family emergency that makes it difficult to close on the agreed-upon date. Having a seller who feels like a partner, and not an adversary, can often smooth over such difficulties.

■ **They possess valuable information about the property.** You might have all the manuals and warranties to appliances, heating and air conditioning units, and other home equipment. But there's still no way you'll be able to instantly understand all the quirks and idiosyncrasies of your new home. It's invaluable to have a friendly seller who's willing to go over the property with you before closing—or who can even be available by phone after you move in.

■ **They have friends and acquaintances in the neighborhood.** You are about to enter a new community. An angry or disgruntled seller could poison the atmosphere before you go to the first block party. Much better to have the seller spreading the good news about the wonderful new occupants!

Get the scoop

Before engaging with a seller, gather as much information as you can. The more you know, the stronger your negotiating position will be.

You've already accomplished a great deal by putting together your CMA and by closely examining the property disclosure form the seller has provided. You may even have hired an independent inspector to examine the property before making your offer. If you can, try to find out even more.

Number one is the reason the sellers have put their home on the market. Perhaps they have a growing family and need a bigger place than the two-bedroom condo they've been living in. Or maybe they're seniors eager to move to Arizona for the weather. Perhaps there's been a divorce, a lost job, or an illness that has stretched the family's financial resources. Although you don't want to take advantage of someone else's misfortune, understanding the seller's motivation can help you formulate a winning negotiation strategy.

How can you find out these things? Just ask. Often, your real estate agent will know the circumstances surrounding the listing. Or you can ask the seller directly. Most won't hesitate to volunteer the information if you ask the question diplomatically. But even if you can't find out why a seller has put their property on the market, there are ways to tell when you have some leverage on your side:

■ **The seller wants a quick closing.** Usually time pressure is a hint that the seller will be motivated to strike a deal sooner rather than later. In a case like this they will also likely be willing to drop the price or make concessions if approached in the right way.

■ **The house has been on the market for longer than similar properties.** Frequently this signals that a seller will be open to proposals. Just make sure you investigate whether there is a problem with the property that is scaring potential buyers off.

- **The price has already been lowered once or more.** This is always a sign that the seller is motivated.

- **The home is empty.** If the current owners have already moved out, chances are they've purchased a home somewhere else. They may have relocated to another state or simply moved across town. Either way, they're probably paying double housing costs until the property is sold. This presents a prime opportunity to negotiate for a better price, better terms, or both.

- **The sellers have a contingency on a property they have purchased.** In this very common scenario, the sellers will have bought another home with the contingency that they sell the current one. These kinds of sellers are highly motivated, as there is probably a time limit on the contingency, after which they will lose the new property.

Win-win negotiations

Rather than simply haggling over price, you can negotiate with sellers in other ways in order to come up with a contract that works for both of you.

- **Share closing/financing costs.** A seller who is unyielding about the property's price might be willing to pay some of the closing or financing costs. This could greatly reduce your out-of-pocket expenses.

- **Cooperate on repairs.** Most sellers will agree to fix specified defects found by the inspection prior to closing. But you might be able to save them the trouble, and yourself some money, by agreeing to take care of the repairs if they lower the price of the house.

- **Shorten/lengthen closing time.** Some sellers have very specific needs when it comes to closing. They may want to close as soon as the next week. Or they may want a 90-day closing period because their new home won't be available until then. Either way, you can often get some concessions or price reductions by being flexible about the closing date.

Watch for the Switcheroo

Be sure to write down the model numbers of the appliances to make sure they aren't switched before closing. You likely didn't purchase the property for the appliances, but you might have been salivating for that brand-new stainless-steel refrigerator—and might have negotiated hard for it. So you should make sure you get what you've contracted for.

Escrow

O nce your offer has been accepted, it's time to write your first check. It will be for the "earnest money" you promised to pay the seller upon signing the contract. But writing the check to the seller personally could lead to trouble. If, for some reason, the transaction can't be completed, you might have difficulty getting your money back. That's why you write your check to an independent third party as a way of establishing *escrow.* At this point in the home-buying process, you will choose a company or individual to act as your *escrow officer.* Depending on where you live, the escrow officer could be a mortgage broker, a private escrow or title insurance company, or a lawyer.

At its most basic level, escrow is established when one person deposits money or other assets of value into an independent account, from which another person will eventually be paid. Before the money—or other asset— is transferred, however, certain specified conditions must be met.

In the case of a real estate transaction, the money placed in escrow includes the earnest money that you have agreed to pay the seller. It also commonly includes the down payment you are making on the mortgage. All this money will be distributed to the appropriate people when the deal has been closed.

The seller also places a valuable asset in escrow: the deed to the property. The independent third party ensures that the deed won't change hands until the seller has received all the money due for the sale.

Escrow is designed to protect all parties involved. Because the escrow officer—usually a representative of an escrow company or a title company—is legally obliged to keep the funds and related documents safe until all conditions have

From Offer to Contract

Before you present an offer, you sign it. If the seller then accepts it and signs it without any changes, you have a legally binding contract. You cannot get out of it without forfeiting your earnest money (unless, of course, some of the specified contingencies are not met). If the seller responds with a counteroffer, your offer is deemed void. But if you sign their counteroffer, it then becomes a contract. Either party can back out before both have signed the contract.

been met, buyers are assured that their money won't disappear before they can take possession of a house, and sellers know that the deeds they submit won't be handed over until they receive full payment for their property.

The escrow officer typically performs a number of other functions too, including processing all loan documents and payments; facilitating the title report; calculating prorations such as insurance, utilities, and property taxes; and paying agreed-upon costs for such things as inspections or completion of repairs.

One very important function that an escrow officer provides is to "clear" the title. The title to a piece of property is simply the ownership. Whoever "holds" title is the owner of the property in question. Sounds simple. But titles can be complicated things. Sellers might say—or even believe—that they hold the title to a piece of property and yet don't. Perhaps someone else from decades before has prior claim on it. Or there may be a "lien" —that's a financial obligation to a lender or a government agency—that means the seller doesn't have the right to sell the property outright. For example, if property owners fail to pay their property taxes, the local county could put a lien against their homes that could legally prevent theme from selling until the debt is paid. In either case, the escrow officer must perform an all-important "title search," which is the process of going through legal records and verifying that the current owner does indeed have the right to sell the property in question.

Quick Tip

No Escrow Referral Fees

Most first-time home buyers wouldn't know where to begin to find an escrow officer, so they depend heavily on referrals from their agents, friends, or families. Most states have laws forbidding the payment of "referral fees" from the escrow company to the referring person in order to ensure that agents and other real estate professionals act in good faith when making recommendations.

As part of the title search, most escrow officers will recommend—and most lenders will require—that you pay for title insurance. This is a special insurance policy that will protect you in case you have to go to court to defend your title. Why get title insurance if the escrow company is performing the search? Simply because there is always a chance that something might be missed, and the last thing you want is the trouble and expense of a lawsuit!

Responsibility for choosing an escrow officer varies from state to state. In some states, the seller (or seller's agent) chooses; in others, the buyer chooses the escrow officer. If it's up to you to choose and you don't know who to select or how, your agent should be able to recommend someone. Then, based on the details of the contract both you and the seller have signed, your respective agents will draw up and deliver detailed instructions to the escrow officer. The escrow officer will then prepare escrow documents that specify all the conditions that need to be met by the closing date. When all these conditions have been met and the money has been paid out and the deed transferred, escrow has officially been "closed."

What Is an Appraisal?

An appraisal is done once the contract is signed. It is an independent assessment performed by the bank to make sure that the property being purchased is indeed worth the purchase price at current market rates. Banks do not want to make a loan for more than a home is actually worth.

Appraisers generally have to be certified by the state. Many offer conservative estimates, especially in seller's markets, where frenzied bidding for homes and multiple offers result in buyers paying more than market value for a property. The appraiser inspects the property and finds out what similar properties have been sold in the immediate geographic area. If the resulting appraisal is quite low compared to those properties, the lender or broker will sometimes do additional research to find comparable properties and argue that the appraisal should be higher. If that doesn't work, the buyer has to come up with the difference between the appraised value of the home and the purchase price.

Hands-on Experience

"*Make sure you get an inspector who has spent a significant amount of time in the field as a contractor. Too many inspectors have gotten their license without having any actual hands-on experience. You want someone who has actually worked as a heating or air condition contractor, or an exterminator, or a plumber. They're the ones who really know their stuff.*"

Maggie Griffin, Realtor,
Weichert Realtors,
Wallingford, Connecticut

Inspect *the* Property

What Is an Inspection?

Once you have a legal contract to purchase your dream property, you're almost home. But there's one last step to take before closing. You need to verify that the property is in good condition—or at least in the condition you believe it to be in. (The seller might already have disclosed problems you agreed to accept in your contract.) There should be no major surprises after you move in. The electrical system should be safe, the plumbing functional, the furnace and air conditioning units operating properly. The only way to confirm this is through an inspection.

An inspection is an examination of the physical structure and all the major systems of a home. It is not an appraisal. That is something the bank undertakes to make sure the value of the property is equal to or greater than the size of the loan it is making. Nor is an inspection a guarantee of the value of the property—or an assurance that nothing will go wrong with it after you move in. An inspection is a *visual*—that is, a nonintrusive—examination of easily accessible aspects of the house to determine their general quality and to ensure that they are currently operational

QUICK TIP

New Homes Need Inspectors, Too

Like older homes, new ones require an in-depth inspection to uncover shoddy workmanship, mistakes in construction, or other defects. You'll almost certainly have a warranty for a new home, but it's far better to catch problems before you close, while you still have leverage with the builder, than have to pester the builder afterwards—or even go to court.

and do not pose any safety danger to the occupants. Items inspected include the roof, walls, ceilings and floors, windows and doors, foundation, heating/cooling systems, and plumbing and electrical systems.

At the heart of home inspections is the concept of "material defect." This is, by law, any problem with the property, or any portion of it, that would have a significant negative impact on the value of the property or create an "unreasonable" risk to people on the land. Inspectors look for material defects that can be discovered without any physically intrusive probing, dismantling, or removal of components.

A general home inspection is not meant to reveal every small problem, nor is it meant to uncover any invisible or hidden defects in a home. (Most minor or cosmetic flaws should be apparent to the buyer without the aid of a professional.) Inspectors won't pull up carpets to examine floor boards—although they may point out the squeaking noise a floor makes when they walk on it or any warping visible through the carpet. They are not authorized to physically disrupt the property in any way (remember, it doesn't yet belong to you).

Always demand a written report of the results of the inspection. This report should detail every feature of the property that was inspected and identify any material defects. Depending on your contract with the inspector, the report can recommend what needs to be done to fix the problem(s) identified or recommend that further, specialized inspections be ordered. It can also contain estimates of the cost of needed repairs.

The home inspection is a critical part of the purchasing process. Under no circumstances should you proceed with a closing until you have a satisfactory inspection report (or reports, if you choose to hire specialists) in hand. You probably have a limited time—the standard provision is two weeks—to complete these inspection(s), so don't waste any time.

The standard inspection contingency in your contract with the seller should give you a clear "out" should anything previously undisclosed or undetected show up on the inspector's report. If this happens, you may simply walk away without losing anything except the check you wrote to the inspector. Or you may decide to try renegotiating your contract with the seller.

Unless the seller has made a specific concession to the contrary in your contract, the buyer pays for any inspections, which typically range in cost from $200 to $800 and can take from two to six hours.

Why Inspect?

Why spend several hundred dollars for a home inspection if the seller has already disclosed everything (as required by most states) and if you have already asked specific questions about important aspects of the property and received the answers in writing?

Two good reasons: First, the seller might not have been completely honest with you. There are sellers who are so anxious to sell at the highest price possible (or at any price at all) that they are willing to omit details or outright lie on their property disclosure statements. Protect yourself against dishonesty by hiring an inspector.

The second reason is that the seller may be unaware of some problems. Perhaps the seller honestly doesn't know about the termites, the leak in the plumbing, or the lead in the well. Ultimately, it doesn't matter whether information about a problem has been innocently or deliberately withheld. You're going to be responsible for the home after closing, and it's important to reduce your risk as much as possible.

Choose an Inspector

H ome inspectors are often contractors who migrated into the profession through hands-on experience in constructing or repairing properties. Most states don't regulate home inspectors. But industry organizations such as the American Society of Home Inspectors (ASHI) and the National Association of Home Inspectors (NAHI) have certification programs that include training courses and exams, and they provide strict codes of conduct. Likewise, most states have some kind of accreditation and/or testing program to make sure home inspectors meet certain minimal requirements.

Find an inspector

The easiest ways to find an inspector are through your agent or word of mouth. Ask your friends, relatives, and co-workers if they know a good inspector. You can also search from your computer on the ASHI website. Type in your zip code and get a list of recommended inspectors in your area. Ask for recommendations. Once you have a few names, there are a number of things you can do to make sure you are engaging a competent professional:

- **Ask for references.** The best predictor of any inspector's future performance is their past record. Get references from at least three previous clients.

- **Check credentials.** Many states require home inspectors to pass exams or work a certain number of hours under a qualified mentor before they are certified. Check

The American Society of Home Inspectors

Founded in 1976, the American Society of Home Inspectors (ASHI) is a nonprofit professional organization for home inspectors dedicated to establishing and advocating high standards of practice and a strict code of ethics for the inspecting community. ASHI currently has more than six thousand members, and its Standards of Practice have been used as the basis for many states' home inspection legislation. In addition to being a resource for inspectors themselves, ASHI's website (*www.ashi. org*) delivers consumer advice for buyers that, among other things, provides them with the ability to find ASHI-certified home inspectors in a particular geographic area.

What an Inspector Won't Check

Inspectors will not be looking at window treatments, wallpaper, or carpets. They'll be examining structural, mechanical, and/or environmental problems, not surface defects that can be corrected through redecorating or cosmetic refinishing.

And keep in mind that the primary inspector you use won't be an expert in everything. You'll almost certainly want a specialized termite inspector, for instance. You may also wish to hire an electrician or plumber if your primary inspector suspects a deeper problem with any of these systems than they can diagnose alone.

the requirements of your particular state at *www.ashi.org/ inspectors/state.asp* and ask the inspector you are considering to provide proof that they have the necessary credentials. If your state doesn't have official requirements, ask your inspector for documentation proving ASHI certification. Ask how many years they've been in business and how many inspections they've performed—expressed both as a lifetime total and as an annual average.

- **Get copies of sample inspection reports.** You'll want evidence that the inspector provides detailed reports in writing and that these reports contain more than a simple checklist saying "acceptable" or "unacceptable." The most useful kind of report will have specific comments on each major structural or system component of the property. It should contain recommendations for fixing any problems, as well estimates of what it will cost to repair them.

- **Verify that the inspector has errors and omissions (E&O) insurance.** This is insurance that the inspector takes out to cover damages arising out of negligence or failure to find all material defects in a property. In the unlikely event that something goes terribly wrong due to an inspector's mistake or incompetence, you want to make sure you'll recover all the expenses required to remedy the situation.

Quick Tip

Go for the Pro

A home inspection must be done by a professional. Don't even think of trying to do it yourself or asking a friend or relative who has a talent for fixing things to do it for you. Your home probably represents the largest and most important investment you are ever going to make in your life. Don't try to cut corners or save a few dollars by using an amateur inspector.

The Inspection

O nce you've chosen an inspector with proven experience and credentials, it's time to schedule the
inspection. The two most important considerations:

■ Schedule the inspection during daylight hours. The
inspection is based on what the inspector can see, not
on any dismantling or deconstructing of any aspect of
the property. So it's essential to do the inspection in
broad daylight.

■ Schedule the inspection for a time when you can go
along. You need to be able to ask questions as the
inspection proceeds, rather than waiting to get what can
sometimes be a report full of contractor's jargon. Even if
you have a nine-to-five job, take the time off to accom-
pany the inspector. In the end, you'll save more time,
and you'll avoid potential misunderstandings.

QUICK TIP

Inspect the Inspection

Although there are generally accepted standards for what a home inspection should include—
particularly in states that regulate the profession—every inspector is different. Some will
examine a roof from a balcony or window, for example, but won't climb on top of it. Ask very
specifically about what will and won't be inspected. Go over the guidelines on pages 152-154
with your inspector, agree on exactly what will be inspected, and get it in writing.

What an inspector should check

An inspection should cover the most important components of a house from top to bottom, inside and out. Be sure your inspector thoroughly examines these features:

■ **Roof.** The inspection should include the roof covering, gutters, downspouts, vents, flashing, and chimney. Although an inspector is not required to walk on the roof, they should closely examine it from the nearest available window, door, or balcony. Some inspectors will get out on top of the house, either as a standard operating procedure or for an extra fee. If this is a non-negotiable item for you, make sure you ask ahead of time if your inspector is willing to do it.

■ **Foundation.** This portion of the inspection should include the basement as well as any crawlspaces under the house and any visible structural aspects of the foundation. The inspector is not required to go into any space that is not easily accessible or to dig around or behind other objects or structures in order to examine anything. As much as possible, however, the inspector should be looking for evidence that water has permeated the foundation or that walls have shifted position.

■ **Exterior.** Is the house in need of exterior repairs or maintenance? What is the condition of siding and flashing? Windows, exterior doors, decks, steps, porches, and railings should be carefully examined. Any trees, bushes, or vines that could potentially affect the structure need to be inspected as well. A basic inspection won't include fences, exterior lights, underground utilities, or anything not readily visible from the ground. If you want those to be included, they have to be separately negotiated in the contract.

■ **Interior.** Inside doors, windows, walls, ceilings, and stairways should all be examined carefully by an inspector, as should garage doors (including electric garage door openers). Door locks should also be examined. Inspectors will generally not look at interior paint, wallpaper, window treatments, or other cosmetic aspects of a house. They will not move furniture or rugs or inspect household appliances. Nor will they inspect pools, spas, hot tubs, or any related components unless asked to do so.

■ **Plumbing.** The inspector should flush all toilets and run water in all sinks and bathtubs. They should also make sure that there is a main water shut-off valve that is easily accessible. All faucets should be in working order. Any sump pumps should drain properly. The type of piping—both internal to the property and running externally to the street main—should be identified and its quality noted. Inspectors won't inspect or judge the age or quality of appliances such as dishwashers or washing machines, nor will they test water quality. Water quality can be tested through an additional, specialized inspection.

■ **Electrical systems.** The external service line to the house, as well as the meter box and main on-off switch, should be included in the inspection. This part of the procedure should confirm the existence of, and easy access to, panels, breakers, and fuses. The inspector should also make sure that the system includes grounding and bonding—and that those components are working. On-off switches to lighting fixtures should be tested, as should all circuit breakers. If aluminum wiring has been used—as was frequently the case for construction completed in the 1960s and 1970s—that needs to be noted. The presence of smoke detectors is mandated by most states, and your inspector should note this. However, they won't take apart any structures to examine the underlying wiring, inspect alarm systems or generators, make sure that breakers have been labeled correctly, or perform intrusive operations on the electrical system.

■ **Heating and cooling systems.** Any controls that the property owner would use to regulate the temperature of the house need to be in working order, as do the heating and cooling systems. In general, inspectors will not examine the inside of a chimney (that requires a specialized inspection), nor will they examine underground fuel tanks or solar energy systems.

- **Ventilation and insulation.** The presence or absence of proper ventilation and insulation should be included in any inspection report. However, the inspector will not go to extreme lengths to enter attics, crawlspaces, or other places that are not easily accessible. Inspectors are generally not qualified to make observations about whether asbestos has been used in insulation or other building materials. Specialized tests are required to establish this.

Additional inspections

In addition to the basic home inspection, most consumer and environmental organizations recommend that the following tests be performed. These usually require hiring specialists, as the majority of general inspectors don't have the knowledge or equipment to perform these functions.

- **Test the water.** Although water from public water supplies is usually tested for toxic substances, it passes through piping that may be aged and contain lead or other hazardous materials that will seep into the water as it passes through them. Alternatively, the plumbing system on the property itself may contain lead. The same risks apply to private wells, as the water feeding those tends to come from the same aquifers that feed local water supplies—which isn't tested at all.

- **Test for radon.** Radon is a poisonous, radioactive gas that has recently been discovered in a significant number of homes, primarily because of poor ventilation. Unfortunately, having a new home doesn't mean the dwelling will be radon-free, as the gas naturally exists in soil and can leak through even well-constructed foundations. Because radon has been classified by the

INSIDER'S INSIGHT

A Second Look

Even though I don't specifically inspect appliances, I will tell a buyer when a piece of equipment is near to the end of its statistical life. If you've got a water heater or air conditioner that is 15 years old, or a roof that is 20 years old, there's a statistical probability that such things will need to be replaced fairly soon. That's different from finding an actual problem, or predicting that it will fail, but it's important information for the buyer nonetheless.

Richard Harmon,
Home Inspector and BBB member,
RMH & Associates, Cleveland, Ohio

Environmental Protection Agency (EPA) as a Class One human lung carcinogen, the U.S. government strongly recommends that all homes be tested for it whenever they change ownership.

■ **Test for lead.** If you are purchasing a home built prior to 1978, you must test for lead, as it was not banned as an ingredient in standard paint until that year. According to some estimates, a whopping 75 percent of all homes contain some lead-based paint. The dangers of lead paint are not limited to small children being poisoned by chewing on windowsills or doorframes. It can also come from the effects of inhaling dust fallout that is undetectable to the naked eye—and which can't be eliminated by vacuuming. Lead is particularly dangerous for children and can lead to brain damage and a host of other neurological problems.

■ **Test for asbestos.** Asbestos is a Class One carcinogen that was banned as an ingredient in building materials in the U.S. in 1987. Today, it is widely known that asbestos fibers increase the risk of lung cancer and other respiratory tract diseases, but a surprising number of buyers don't bother to have asbestos testing done on older homes. Don't take anyone's word that the property you are buying is free of asbestos. Hire an experienced inspector to check whether this is true or not.

INSIDER'S INSIGHT

Termite Tips

Frequently, a home has already been treated for termites. You should ask what kind of chemicals the termite company has used—there are a number of them out there—and how they have been applied. There are various non-chemical termite treatments as well that are generally found in newer construction, that can be attractive to families with young children or pets.

Pat Perelli, Realtor and BBB member,
John Hall & Associates,
Phoenix, Arizona

The Report

After your inspector finishes examining the property, you should receive a detailed report. Make sure that this comes in written form. There's no way you could absorb every bit of information during a verbal summary, and if anything serious is found, you'll need to submit documentation about it to the seller.

If the inspector's report comes back clean, you can proceed to closing. But if any problems have been uncovered, you have four options:

■ **Ignore the problem.** Yes, you can do this. Perhaps you're tired of looking for properties, putting in offers, and negotiating, and you just want to take possession. Perhaps you know you have a good enough deal on the property or that the sellers have already been financially pushed to the limit of what they can concede. Or maybe it's a seller's market and if you threaten to walk away from the deal, the homeowner will have plenty of others vying to purchase the property.

■ **Ask the seller to fix the problem.** This is probably the most common course of action. Take a copy of the inspection report to the seller (or the seller's agent) and say you need to have the problems fixed before you will proceed with the deal. The seller can always refuse. They may do this if there were multiple offers and the seller accepted backup offers from other would-be buyers. In this case, you can threaten to walk away from the deal. After all, you've probably negotiated that right via an inspector's contingency in the contract. But you're unlikely to have much leverage if others are standing in line. In a buyer's market, you'll have more leverage, of course.

■ **Renegotiate the price and take care of the repairs yourself.** Whether the seller will agree to this depends on the type of market you are in and how motivated they are to sell. A seller who cannot afford to make the repairs will push for this resolution. If the inspector has included estimates of how much it will cost to repair identified problems, you have a good basis for negotiating a discount on the contracted price of the house. If not, you'll have to call up contractors and gather bids yourself. It's a good idea to take this extra step so you're not surprised by the cost of fixing a leaking roof or a sagging window frame.

■ **Walk away from the deal.** If you've included the all-important inspection contingency in your contract, you can decide that the problems are too extensive and you'd rather cut your losses and find a less challenging property to buy.

INSIDER'S INSIGHT
Full Disclosure

"One thing that a buyer has in his or her favor is that once a defect has been uncovered by an inspector, the seller will be obligated to disclose it to all other potential buyers. So you have a certain amount of leverage, because if you walk away from the deal, the next buyer will probably make similar demands that the problem either be fixed or the property price discounted."

Kenneth Etter,
Broker and BBB member,
Kenneth Etter Realty,
Reno, Nevada

The Most Common House Repair Problems

Although an inspection can uncover any number of problems, major flaws are most frequently found in these areas:

■ **Roofing.** Although the homeowner was almost certainly required by state regulations to disclose the age of the roof, as well as any leaks or obvious defects, sometimes a "resurfaced" roof—that is, one where additional roofing materials were placed on top of existing materials—may have problems that are more difficult to find. Previously undetected issues in a resurfaced roof are exceedingly common and can cost many thousands of dollars to fix, particularly if underlying layers need to be removed before new materials are put on.

■ **Basement.** Basements that flood when it rains frequently appear on inspector's reports and can be very expensive to fix. Although you can waterproof a basement with a sump pump, the cost will be significant and should be the responsibility of the seller. You'll have to pay, however, if you knew about the defect before you signed the contract and waived any contingencies related to it.

■ **Insulation.** Inadequate insulation, particularly in older homes, is a widespread problem. The result can be exorbitant energy bills in both summer and winter.

■ **Structure**. Frequently a standard inspection will uncover irregularities in the roof, exterior wall, or interior framing of the house that will eventually require repair work totaling tens of thousands of dollars. In a worst-case scenario, you might have to jack up a house to repair such defects. You may have grounds to sue either the seller or the inspector if a major structural problem went unnoticed until after closing. But you probably don't want the hassle and expense of a lawsuit to add to the other stressors involved in taking possession of a property.

■ **Heating.** The most common problem found here is defective heat/air conditioning ducts that can cost many thousands of dollars to fix.

■ **Water.** The top concern related to plumbing is the type of pipe that delivers water from the city- or town-owned main and the property's own plumbing system. Lead or galvanized steel pipes are potentially hazardous and are expensive to replace. Interior pipes need to be examined for leaks or to find out whether root systems have infiltrated. Make sure your inspector verifies that water pressure is acceptable and that all drains are functional. A slow-draining sink or bathtub could be the sign of serious plumbing problems further down the road.

■ **Electrical system.** Electrical systems often fail to meet current standards. There may not be enough switches and outlets, for example. Aluminum wiring installed in the 1960s and 1970s poses particular safety dangers, and rewiring is one of the most expensive repair jobs to perform.

■ **General maintenance.** One of the problems that's likely most familiar to inspectors is a house that has been poorly maintained—or maintained by a do-it-yourselfer without adequate skills. It can take many thousands of dollars to undo amateur attempts to fix or install complex electrical or plumbing systems.

Satisfy Your Curiosity

"*Closings are scary because there are a million things that happen behind the scenes, and you often have no idea what's going on. Make sure you ask your escrow officer about anything you need to make you feel more comfortable with the process. Any good one will take the time to answer your questions.*"

Brad Weber,
Realtor and Broker, AA Realty,
Eagan, Minnesota

Close *the* Deal

What Is a Closing?

C losing is the last step you'll take to make a property your own. It's the scheduled meeting during which the money for the real estate is paid in full to the seller, and the title—or ownership of the property—is transferred to the buyer. The date of the closing is typically also the date when legal possession of the property is physically transferred from the seller to the buyer. This transfer of possession ends with the seller handing over the keys to the house, condominium, or co-op.

When you opened escrow, you hired a title or escrow company to act as an independent facilitator of the completion of the contract. Typically, the closing takes place at the offices of the escrow officer. Depending on where you live, the buyer and seller might both be present at the closing or they might go to the escrow office at different times to sign the documents. The closing date will have been specified in the contract.

QUICK TIP

Limits of Escrow Officers

It's important to understand that escrow officers are not there to protect you against any fraudulent or incorrect information provided by the seller of the property. Their job is to get information from the relevant parties—the bank, the seller, and the buyer—and communicate among them, not to guarantee that any of the documents provided reflect the truth. This is why you always do a final walkthrough *before* closing,

A variety of costs are associated with the transaction. These are called "closing costs," and they include everything from the fees associated with applying for and processing your mortgage to the commissions paid to the buyer's and seller's agents. Who pays for what depends on a combination of local custom and the terms specified in the contract. Sometimes the buyer is responsible for all closing costs. More commonly, the closing costs are split between the buyer and the seller. (See pages 166-168 for more on closing costs.)

The point of the closing

All of this might seem both complicated and unnecessary. After all, the contract has been signed by both parties and you've paid the earnest money signifying your intent to go through with the deal. Why not just hand over a check in exchange for the deed and the keys?

In a word: *security*. Everyone has interests to protect. Bringing everyone and everything together for the closing in a neutral place supervised by an independent party (the escrow officer) ensures that those interests will be protected.

■ **Your interests.** You've already paid your earnest money, which can range from 1 percent to as much as 15 percent of the price of the property. You're now ready to sign mortgage documents that commit you to repaying what could be hundreds of thousands of dollars. Without the supervision of a neutral third party, you could sign all the documents only to have the seller withhold the deed—or hand over a deed that has not been properly researched and cleared, verifying that the property is actually theirs to sell. You have too much at stake to trust to the goodwill of strangers.

■ **The seller's interests.** The seller is about to sign over the ownership rights to a property. To do so without assurances that they will be paid for it would be foolish.

INSIDER'S INSIGHT

Take the Mystery Away

Realtors are really only qualified to provide the basic background on closing. They can't provide legal advice. For that, you need a real estate attorney, who can explain what the papers mean, what you're signing, and what you should watch out for.

Noah Seidenberg,
Agent, Coldwell Banker,
Evanston, Illinois

What if the final check doesn't clear? What if the bank denies the loan at the last minute—after title has already been transferred? The closing process ensures that the funds are in place and immediately accessible upon signing over of the deed.

■ **The agents' interests.** Both your agent and the seller's agent have put in a great deal of work brokering this deal. Their fees have been specified in the contract, and they need assurances that those fees will indeed be paid upon completion of the transaction. The escrow officer collects the fees as part of the closing costs and pays them out once the deal has been completed.

■ **The lender's interests.** The risk to the lender is that the title might not be clear—that is, that the seller doesn't actually have the right to sell the property. If there are any claims on the property later, the loan could be in jeopardy. The title company's assurances that the title is valid are essential to protecting the lender's interests.

QUICK TIP

Getting Legal Advice

Depending on where you live, you might already have involved a lawyer in the home-buying process. But in many states, real estate agents and escrow officers handle everything themselves. Still, if there's any time you should get legal advice, it's during closing. The paperwork is so immense and the legal terms so daunting that it's easy to feel overwhelmed. So it can be well worth the money to have an attorney look over all the documentation before you sign.

Before closing can proceed

Your contract will specify a number of conditions that must be fulfilled before closing can be completed. Among the most important:

■ **Financing.** Your contract will have given you a certain amount of time to secure financing. Your final approval for the mortgage amount and the payment of the agreed down payment to be placed in escrow *must* have occurred before the specified close of escrow date. The lender will also have delivered the mortgage documents you needed to sign to the escrow officer prior to the date of scheduled closing. Additionally, the funds the lender is delivering that will allow you to buy the house need to be in the escrow account before closing can be completed.

■ **Homeowner's insurance.** As part of your agreement with the lender, you will likely be required to obtain homeowner's insurance before the loan can be official. Homeowner's insurance generally includes protections against loss of the home itself and of its contents due to events such as fires. The cost of homeowner's insurance varies depending on how much it would cost to replace the home. The insurance documents will be extremely specific about what will and will not be paid in the case of various events. Typically, Acts of God such as floods and earthquakes require special insurance. Depending on where the property is located, the lender might require flood, earthquake, or other special kinds of insurance.

■ **Title search.** The title company you hired upon opening escrow is responsible for doing comprehensive research on the title. Generally, the search is performed to ensure two things. First, that the seller indeed has the right to sell the property in question, and second, that there are no liens, or claims, that need to be paid off before closing. A lien can be placed against a property by someone to whom the seller still owes money—mortgage payments or back taxes, for instance, as well as other assessments that haven't been settled by the seller.

■ **Title insurance.** The lender typically requires the buyer to acquire title insurance so that the buyer will be protected in case of any after-sale problems resulting from a poor or incomplete title search.

The Deed

One of the most important documents you will receive after closing is the *deed*—the piece of paper that officially delivers ownership of the property from the seller to you. A deed is different from the title in that the deed is the piece of paper that *documents* the title. In other words, even if you lost the deed, you would still have title to the property. (You just might have to jump through hoops to prove it.) Once closing is completed, the deed still needs to be recorded in the appropriate local government office (see page 179).

Who Comes to the Closing?

Who actually shows up at the escrow company's offices on closing day? That varies from state to state. At the very least, all the buyers whose names will be on the deed need to be present, as well as their agent(s) and the escrow officer. Occasionally the seller's agent will be present; more rarely, the seller. If an attorney has been involved, they will also frequently be there in order to make sure that nothing occurs at the last minute to prevent the sale from going through. And some buyers like to have emotional backup as well, so they invite friends or family members to come along, either to provide support or just to celebrate the occasion.

■ **Additional repairs or other material concessions promised by the seller.** In your contract you may have required the seller to fix problems with the property before completion of the sale. These repairs—a new roof, replacement of a rotting deck, or termite eradication— must be completed before you sign the final paperwork.

Closing costs

Until now, the only money you've paid is your earnest money, which was placed in escrow to establish your sincerity and goodwill when you signed the contract. At the closing, you are expected to provide the rest of what you've contractually agreed to pay. This includes the down payment for the mortgage, as well as any application and processing fees or other costs of completing the home-buying process.

You should review the closing costs carefully. Although the truth-in-lending documents and your contract should specify precisely what you will pay in advance, it is not unheard of for lenders and/or title companies to slip in last-minute fees. While the types of closing costs vary from locale to locale and between various types of loans and lenders, you should expect some standard fees:

■ **Down payment.** This should come as no surprise, as you agreed to put down a certain amount of money to secure your loan. Verify that this amount is what you agreed to in your mortgage contract.

■ **Points.** Points are prepaid interest on your mortgage. The lender should have made clear in the mortgage documents what points you were expected to pay on the loan. Again, check that the figures match.

■ **Loan origination fee.** Depending on the type of mortgage you secured, you may have been charged a fee for processing the loan. If this wasn't made clear, or if the fee was not included in the written estimate you received from the mortgage company, you should not sign the documents until this is clarified.

- **Loan processing fees.** Like loan origination fees, these are by no means standard with each type of mortgage. Frequently, processing fees are waived by the lender or mortgage broker. Whether or not you agreed to pay processing fees should be clear from the mortgage documents presented to you.

- **Prepaid interest.** Generally, the lender will require that you prepay interest on the loan from the date of closing until the beginning of the next month. (This is generally when your first mortgage payment is due.)

- **Appraisal fee.** Unless specifically waived in your contract, your lender will charge you for the cost of the property appraisal they performed to make sure the property was indeed worth what you are paying for it.

- **Prepaid mortgage insurance.** If you put down less than 20 percent on a property, a lender will usually require you to obtain mortgage insurance. Your closing costs will include some percentage of the total amount due for the first 6 to 12 months of insurance.

- **Prepaid property insurance.** Your lender will probably require you to pay for a certain percentage of the first year's worth of property insurance.

- **Property taxes (in advance).** Depending on your locale or state, you will frequently be asked to pay a percentage of property taxes in advance of their official due date.

- **Title insurance.** This protects you, and the lender, from any liens or other claims against the property that weren't uncovered by the title search.

- **Recording fees.** These fees cover the notarized recording of the deed.

- **Transfer charges.** Each locale—including state, county, and state jurisdiction—has fees for transferring the title from the seller to the buyer. These fees can range from less than $5 to more than $1,200.

How to Pay Closing Costs

You'll not likely be allowed to pay your closing costs (including down payment) with a personal check. Have a money order or cashier's check prepared in advance. The exact amount you pay should be the number you've come up with in the worksheet on page 168— or the amount your escrow officer has told you to take to their offices on closing day. If you discover any discrepancies, do not proceed until they have been resolved.

■ **Title company/escrow company fees.** The escrow officer doesn't work for free. You will be charged for establishing and processing escrow.

Closing Costs

It's a good idea to go through all the documents before closing and identify the fees you are being charged. Then enter them into the worksheet below. This way, you'll have all the fees in one place and you can verify that you're being charged only once for each item and that the charges are in line with what you should expect. Make sure to run this worksheet past your agent after you've filled it out, and take the it with you to the escrow company's offices on closing day.

FEE	AMOUNT
Down payment	
Points	
Loan origination fee	
Loan processing fee	
Prepaid interest	
Appraisal fee	
Prepaid mortgage insurance	
Prepaid property insurance	
Property taxes (in advance)	
Recording fees	
Title insurance	
Transfer charges	
Title company/escrow company fees	
Total	

The Final Walkthrough

Y our final walkthrough won't take place in the presence of the escrow officer, but it's an essential step in the closing. It will ensure that you're getting what you paid for. Be sure to include a provision for it in your contract. The later you can schedule this walkthrough, the better. The ideal time is 24 hours before the planned closing time and—most importantly—*after* the seller has moved out. As you go through the property, be sure to:

- **Check the general condition of the home.** Is it in the same condition as when you last visited? Be sure that there are no holes in the walls, no new rips or stains in the carpets, no new scratches on the floor.

- **Make sure all concessions have been fulfilled.** Ask for documentation that repairs have been made, such as invoices from contractors. If substantial repairs were made to the plumbing or electrical systems, hire an inspector to ensure that they were done correctly.

  If the seller agreed to leave lighting fixtures, furniture, window coverings, or other items, verify that those are still in place. It is not uncommon for sellers to wait until the last moment to remove things they previously agreed to leave behind.

- **Get proof that appliances haven't been switched— and that they work.** If you wrote down the serial numbers of the major appliances and put them in the contract, you have a way to check that the appliances haven't been switched. Now make sure they're working. This means running the washer, dryer, and dishwasher.

Open the taps to make sure the hot water heater is working. Crank the thermostat to check that the heating and cooling systems are operational and turn the light switches on and off in every room.

- **Verify that all personal possessions of the seller have been removed.** The last thing you want to find when you open the door of your new home is the previous owner's junk. If your property includes storage areas, garages, or outlying buildings, inspect those to make sure all items have been removed.

Your Punch List

Make a list of all the repairs and concessions that are in the contract and check them off as you do your final walkthrough. If any of these items have not been completed, you should *not* proceed with closing. Instead, let your escrow officer know that important conditions of the contract have not been fulfilled. You will generally have the choice of postponing closing or doing some last-minute negotiations with the seller.

WHAT TO LOOK FOR	COMPLETED

If something is wrong

Say there is a problem—holes in the wall where pictures once hung or deep scratches in the floor where something heavy was dragged out the door. What if appliances are missing or broken or there are other failures to live up to contractual promises made during negotiations? Do *not* confront the sellers. Instead, go to your agent immediately and give them a detailed list of all the problems you've uncovered. It's then the agent's job to contact the seller and/or the seller's agent and explain that the conditions must be met before closing can be completed.

At this point the seller has two options if closing is to proceed. They can fix the problem—put back the appliances, fix the holes in the walls, remove their junk—or agree to take money off the closing price so you can take care of the problem yourself. Whatever you decide should be put in writing. Do not sign the final papers until you're sure the conditions have been met.

Procrastinators

If the seller hasn't moved out by the time of your final walkthrough, do *not* proceed to closing. It can be difficult to judge the condition of a property when it is still filled with furniture and boxes. You'll also have no assurance that the property won't be damaged during move-out or that appliances and other concessions will still be there when you actually take possession. Occasionally, a less-than-honest seller might decide to stay in the property for a few days, or even weeks, and once you have closed, there is little you can do beyond taking legal action to evict. Make sure your contract specifies that the seller must move out before your final walkthrough.

To Do's before Closing

Although the escrow officer is in charge of making sure everything is in place prior to closing, you should also be checking that you've fulfilled your end of the bargain. (You can check through your agent, if you're more comfortable that way.) Here's a short checklist that you can use to make sure that you won't be holding up the closing.

TO DO	DATE DONE
Financing secured (commitment letter from lender)	
Homeowner's insurance	
Title search completed	
Title insurance acquired	
Punch list accounted for	
Down payment money on hand	
Final walkthrough completed	

The Closing

The closing generally takes place in the offices of the title or escrow company on a date and time specified in the contract. Four basic steps need to be taken before the closing is complete and escrow can be closed:

■ Review and sign loan documents

■ Review, sign, and exchange documents with the other participants in the transaction (the seller, the lender, and the title/escrow company)

■ Transfer the funds

■ Get the keys from the seller

Expect the closing to take some time. Allow at least a few hours. You'll be signing a large number of documents and you don't want to feel rushed.

Review and sign loan documents

You've received preapproval and final approval of your mortgage. Now it's time to finalize your agreement with the lender to borrow the agreed-upon sum. Expect to sign a number of standard documents:

■ **Truth-in-lending statement.** The Truth in Lending Act (TILA) is a federal law passed to protect consumers. It requires lenders to provide clear disclosure of key terms and costs, including specifying the maximum interest rate on variable rate mortgages.

Do Your Homework

On closing day you won't have time to read through all the documents you'll have to sign, so arrange to get them a day or so before. Read them carefully, and if you have any questions, write them down so you can ask your agent or the escrow officer for clarification before signing. For extra assurance, hire a lawyer to review any documents you don't understand.

■ **Mortgage documents.** These are the final documents you'll have to sign, agreeing to the amount and terms of the mortgage. The figures in the documents will include the total amount of the loan, as well as the amount of interest to be paid over the life of the loan.

■ **Closing costs documents.** You will also be asked to sign documents in which you agree to the various closing costs of the transaction. Examine them carefully to make sure they are in compliance with the terms of the contract you agreed to.

■ **Escrow statement letter.** This document verifies that you will provide sufficient funds to pay for a specified percentage of property taxes and insurance in advance as required by the lender.

QUICK TIP

Signing Your Mortgage Papers

Unless your lender is also your escrow officer, you won't be signing your mortgage papers at the bank. Instead, all the papers will be delivered to your escrow company, and you'll sign them there, along with all the other documents.

Review, sign, and exchange documents with other parties

Once you've signed the loan documents and finalized your agreement with the bank, you'll start signing the paperwork regarding the financial arrangements between everyone else. This includes the agreements between the seller and the buyer, the seller and the title company, the seller and the escrow company, and the buyer and all those parties. Although the precise number and type of documents varies from locale to locale and transaction to transaction, you can expect to see a number of standard forms:

■ **Deed.** A contract doesn't transfer ownership of the property from the seller to the buyer. A separate document, called the deed, is needed for that. As the buyer, you are responsible for providing the full price of the property in exchange for the deed, which should contain the names of all the new owners. So your name will be on the deed, as well as the names of any joint owners, such as a spouse or domestic partner.

- **Deed of trust.** The deed of trust is a deed given by the borrower (you) to a lender in order to secure the mortgage on a property. In most states, a deed creates a lien and not a title transfer, regardless of its terms. In other words, a deed of trust is your legal commitment to the lender that the property will belong to it if you cannot pay back the loan and the mortgage is therefore foreclosed.

- **Escrow documents.** These verify the amounts you will prepay for taxes, insurance, and earnest money escrow.

- **The Real Estate Settlement Procedure Act (RESPA) statement.** Signing this statement verifies that you've been fully briefed on the closing process by your agent, lender, and/or escrow officer.

- **IRS forms.** Various federal and state laws require the title or escrow company to send documents concerning your purchase of the property to the IRS and state taxing authorities.

- **Sanity documents.** You will sign a document or several documents attesting to being of sound mind when completing this transaction.

- **Concession documents.** These include any documentation of escrow payments that were prorated—such as tax or utility bills—or anything else specified in the contract as needing proof of completion.

- **Bill of sale.** This legal document, signed by the seller and given to the buyer, reports that on a specific date, at a specific locality, and for a particular sum of money, the seller sold to the purchaser a property of which he or she had lawful possession.

■ **Title affidavit.** A written statement, made under oath by the seller and acknowledged by a notary public, in which the seller identifies himself or herself and indicates marital status; certifies that since the examination of the title no further liens have been incurred; and certifies that he or she is in possession of the property.

Transfer the funds

At the closing, you will hand over your money order or cashier's check for the remainder of the money due. This will include the down payment for the mortgage minus your earnest money, any payments for insurance or property taxes specified in the contract, and any closing costs you have agreed to cover. The seller will also provide a check for any closing costs they have agreed to cover. Your mortgage company will also have placed the money for the loan into your escrow account—generally by wire transfer. The escrow agent will then distribute the money to each party as specified: the seller will be paid for the property, the agents will be paid their commissions, the title company and any other parties to the transaction, such as attorneys, will be paid their agreed-upon fees.

Hand over the keys

Once all funds have been distributed and the papers signed and notarized, the seller, their agent, or the escrow officer will hand the keys to you, and you will then be in legal possession of the house. At this point, the closing is considered complete, and escrow is closed. You are now the owner of your new home!

If You Want to Back Out Now …

It's unusual, but not unheard of, for a buyer to get cold feet at the last minute. What happens if you decide that, for whatever reason—emotional or financial—you can't go through with the deal? For starters, you will lose your earnest money. And in most states, the seller might be able to successfully sue you for breach of contract, which means the courts can force you to go through with the contract.

In most cases, sellers won't proceed legally—after all, they'll have a lot of hassle and expense if they go that route. Instead, they'll take the earnest money and put the property back on the market. The loss to you can be considerable, especially if you've put down 5 or 15 percent of the property price.

If Closing Is Delayed

Few things are more disappointing than looking forward to the end of the home-buying process only to have it delayed for days, or even weeks, until problems are resolved. There may even be practical complications. What if you've given notice at your rental apartment and have to be out immediately?

Unfortunately, you have few options except to push for any issues to be resolved as quickly as possible. This is why you should always build in a buffer around your closing date. Arrange for a one- or even two-week overlap between the end of your current living situation and your official move-in to your new property. It's also a good idea to have some extra money in the bank to pay for a hotel or other living arrangement in case things go really wrong!

What could go wrong?

If anything goes wrong … be assertive! In no circumstances should you proceed with the closing until you are comfortable with the state of the property and certain that the financial arrangements have been made as promised. Some common closing difficulties:

- **Walkthrough problems.** If you discover problems during your final walkthrough, you have two choices: to proceed with the closing or to demand that the seller meet their obligations before you sign the final documents. If the apparent breach of contract is considerable, such as the failure to fix a major electrical problem, delay closing until the repair is done or until the seller agrees to make an appropriate financial settlement. But you may choose to let lesser matters go in order to gain possession of the house sooner rather than later.

- **Cash problems.** Sometimes a buyer cannot come up with the amount needed to close the deal. In such cases, the ball is in the seller's court. They can agree to give the buyer more time or even finance the difference—or they can walk away from the deal. In rare cases, a seller might even choose to sue. What happens depends on the temperament of the seller—and on the relationship you have forged with them during the negotiating and signing of the contract. This is an excellent reason to keep negotiations civil and to strive for a win-win situation.

- **Loan problems.** Occasionally something will go wrong with the financing at the last minute. Problems can range from incorrect information on the loan documents— such as typos or incorrect addresses—to the bank not getting the actual documents or money to the escrow officer in time. You might also find things in the final documents, such as unanticipated closing costs, that you refuse to pay. Until these points are settled, the closing cannot continue.

■ **Title problems.** It's the title company's responsibility to do a title search and clear the title for transfer from the seller to you. But sometimes, at the last moment, things come up that complicate matters. No matter what the seller says to convince you otherwise, refuse to sign any closing documents until you have assurances of a clear title.

■ **Occupancy problems.** Unless otherwise agreed upon, do not sign any closing documents until the seller is out of the house. If you are purchasing property that has been used for rental, do not sign until the tenants have left. Closing before a property is vacant is asking for trouble, as any leverage you have to get occupants out disappears once the seller receives his or her money.

INSIDER'S INSIGHT

Getting the Date Right

"Make sure you have the words 'on or before' when specifying the date of the closing. Otherwise, without that phrase, the closing can take place anytime 10 days before or 10 days after the date mentioned in the contract."

Maggie Griffin, Realtor,
Weichert Realtors,
Wallingford, Connecticut

Take Possession

ossession is legally defined as having some degree of control over something else. You gain possession of the property when you have the keys and control over access to and from a home.

Closing and possession are not the same thing. Occasionally, as part of the terms of the contract, a buyer might agree with the seller to postpone possession of the house. If a seller asks for extra time, it's usually because their new home is not yet available. In such cases, you should negotiate a daily or weekly rate that the seller must pay after closing has been completed. If your seller does ask for more time, the rate you calculate should be based on *all* your costs, including your mortgage payments, account utilities, property taxes, and insurance.

It's less common for the buyer to ask the seller if they can move in before closing. This happens when the buyer needs to be out of a rental property by a certain date, and there is a gap between that date and closing. The seller might agree to this concession if they have already moved out of the property in question. In such cases, a rental fee will be negotiated, based on the same factors you would use if the seller asked to stay on after closing.

QUICK TIP

Keep Those Documents Safe!

If you don't yet have a safe deposit box, now is the time to get one. Every single document given to you as part of your purchase should be put there so you can find them easily, whether for filing tax returns or selling the property in the future.

Handing over the keys

This final step must be taken before closing is complete, and it's not just a formality. More often than you might imagine, keys don't work or they don't unlock all the doors, storage facilities, or mailboxes. Because the exchange of keys is a good-faith transaction, you are forced to trust that the seller will provide all the keys, and the right keys, and that they will work. If for some reason anything goes wrong, you'll have little recourse but to call a locksmith and fork over the money to remove the old locks and install new ones.

Recording the deed

The deed is the document that proves the bearer has title to a particular property. As part of the sale process, the deed is transferred from the seller to you, the buyer. Your name and address are then put on the deed, and the transfer must then be recorded by your local Office of County Recorder.

Sometimes the title company will record the deed for you; sometimes you have to take the deed to the recording office yourself. In either case, recording the deed is an essential step in home ownership, as it becomes part of the public record, and all property tax bills are subsequently sent to the address listed on the deed.

Keep Phone Numbers Handy

Once you have the keys to the house, the home-buying process is theoretically over. But in reality, problems do come up after closing. Perhaps you can't locate the key to the storage shed. Or you may have misplaced the warranty information for the appliances that the seller included in the sale. In such cases, you'll want to keep the phone numbers of your agent, the seller's agent, and—if possible—the seller handy. Post them by your phone so you can find them in a hurry.

QUICK TIP

Break Open the Champagne!

The moment you use your newly acquired keys to open the front door of your home is truly exciting, and it's one that you should celebrate. Many first-time buyers break open special bottles of wine or champagne, have picnics in their as-yet-unfurnished home, or throw parties before the furniture has arrived! Whatever you do, try to savor the moment—it's one you'll look back on for many years to come!

Get Financial Counseling

" There are many programs for first-time investors in which a financial consultant or mortgage lender will help you get into a rental property with a relatively small amount of money down, as long as you will have a positive cash flow from the rental income. "

Maggie Griffin, Realtor,
Weichert Realtors,
Wallingford, Connecticut

Buying *for* Investment

Why Purchase Rental Property?

Renovation Remedies

Many lenders offer low-interest financing programs for rental property owners who need to make major renovations. Investigate such programs if you know you'll need to replace the roof, paint the exterior, fix the plumbing, or incur another large expense.

W hen people buy homes, they don't always plan to live there themselves. They may choose to enter the housing market by purchasing residential or commercial property to rent or lease to others. The decision to purchase investment property involves more than just financial considerations. It's also a practical and *emotional* choice. Are you cut out to be a landlord? Are you prepared to assume the responsibilities of dealing with tenants and repairs and handling emergencies? Whether you're buying residential or commercial property, being a landlord takes time and money. Each type of property offers its own benefits—and challenges:

■ **Residential rental property.** A residential property has tenants who use it as a residence (but not for commercial or industrial purposes). Properties must be zoned residential in order to be used in this way, although some properties have dual zoning provisions that allow for both residential and commercial uses (as in the case of live-work lofts). There are two kinds of residential properties: single-family homes and multi-unit dwellings, or MUDs. Single-family homes are meant to be occupied by one person, a married couple, two domestic partners, a family, or a contracted number of unrelated persons (as permitted under local regulations) who have agreed to share a single living space (roommates, for example). MUDs are buildings that contain two or more separate living units. Apartment houses are the most common types of MUDs.

The benefit of owning residential property is that the residential rental market is generally less volatile than the commercial rental market. It's true that if the economy is doing poorly and employers leave an area, there are likely to be higher vacancy rates in residential rentals. But in general, the residential rental market is more stable and the income stream more predictable. On the other hand, you are likely to have higher turnover in a residential unit than in a commercial unit, especially in areas with a high transient population, such as a college town.

- **Commercial rental property.** Tenants in a commercial property use it to conduct businesses ranging from restaurants to bicycle shops to accounting operations or psychotherapy practices. The premises can be anything from a small store to an office in a gigantic office complex. Depending on the zoning, the tenants may or may not be able to use their locations for industrial applications, such as manufacturing, mechanical repairs, or shop work. Unless specified otherwise by city or county zoning laws, tenants are not allowed to live in these places of work. The advantage of owning commercial property over residential property is that the income tends to be much higher on a per-square-foot basis, leases tend to be longer in duration, and turnover less high. However, vacancies, when they occur, can last much longer. Other challenges arise from having to provide the infrastructure for a business. Commercial tenants can be even more demanding than residential ones because their livelihood depends on having their premises in good working order.

The Live-In Landlord

Purchasing a multi-unit dwelling (MUD) and living in one of the units yourself has a number of advantages. For starters, the rental income from the other units usually covers the operating costs of maintaining the property and often a large part of the mortgage. You'll also be on the scene to monitor the property, and you'll be able to take care of any problems that arise immediately, rather having to rely on a tenant to report a problem. Tenants who are looking for a place to throw parties or deal drugs will be discouraged if they know the owner is on site, so you can usually attract a higher quality of renter. One enormous advantage of a MUD is that you can usually get a less expensive "owner-occupied" loan if you're willing to live in one of your units. This often helps first-time buyers qualify for bigger properties in better neighborhoods.

The National Real Estate Investors Association

The National Real Estate Investors Association (*http://www. nationalreia.com*) is a non-profit trade federation made up of local rental property owner associations and investment clubs throughout the U. S. Representing investor, property owner, apartment, and landlord associations on a national scale, the NREIA provides training, conferences, publications, peer-to-peer support, a code of ethics, legal information, and other informational services to individual investors. The NREIA offers a wide array of resources to help you purchase and manage rental property.

The benefits of owning rental property

Although people purchase their own homes hoping to reap good returns on their investment, when purchasing rental property, that is your *sole* goal. Unless you plan to live in part of the property yourself (and rent out the rest) you will not have the pleasure of calling the place home while it appreciates. Instead, your financial goals are an end in themselves. Indeed, many people decide that rental property will be the cornerstone of their long-term financial plan—in effect, they are choosing to invest in real estate instead of the stock or bond market. Some of the financial benefits of doing this include:

- **Generating positive cash flow.** Once you've pulled together the down payment—which is likely to be substantially more than what's required for a home you'd live in yourself (see page 192)—you'll get an influx of cash every month when your tenants pay their rent. If you set your rental prices correctly, you should be able to realize a positive cash flow even after you subtract operating expenses.

- **Securing a free place to live.** If you purchase a property that allows you to live on the premises, you can effectively live for free. This can be especially attractive in locations where the cost of housing is high.

- **Getting tax breaks.** Even if you have a positive cash flow, you may find yourself operating at a net loss once you consider depreciation and mortgage interest deductions. Depending on your income bracket, you can deduct that loss from your income tax, resulting in tax savings.

- **Benefiting from the property's long-term appreciation.** Although multiple-unit properties generally do not appreciate as quickly as single-family homes, a well-maintained building in a good neighborhood should increase in value over time.

The drawbacks of owning rental property

Despite all the potential financial benefits, purchasing a rental property presents a number of drawbacks. Many of these have to do with your personal comfort zone. Are you suited to be a landlord? Are you content to continue renting your primary residence for an undetermined length of time to come? Before you proceed, consider the risks of owning rental property:

- **Delay in owning a home of your own.** If your financial resources are limited, you will probably tie up a high proportion of them in your investment property. This will prevent you from purchasing a dream home of your own, and you'll have to continue renting—or living with friends or relatives—for the foreseeable future.

- **The possibility that the property doesn't appreciate.** When you purchase your own home, the pleasure of living in it yourself is a major benefit. With a rental property, you are interested only in its investment potential. If the property fails to appreciate, you may not realize your goals.

- **Loss of cash if property is unoccupied.** If your rental property remains empty for as little as a month or two, you can lose significant amounts of cash.

- **Legal expenses.** If you rent to a bad tenant who doesn't pay the rent but refuses to move out, you may have to resort to costly eviction procedures.

- **Assuming the responsibilities and liabilities of being a landlord.** Some people simply aren't suited to be landlords. Taking on landlord duties if you fall into this category can be emotionally—and financially—very painful and not worth the trouble.

- **Having a negative cash flow.** If the market won't bear sufficiently high rents or if the current tenants' rents are fixed by leases or rent-control laws, you might actually lose money every month.

Does Buying a Rental Property Make Sense?

 comparative market analysis (CMA), where one home is compared with similar homes on the basis of size, features, location, and "extras" is the standard tool for determining the value of an owner-occupied house. The process for determining the value of rental property is slightly different. Both the prevailing market prices for similar properties and the condition of the property itself play a huge part in determining its value. But whether a specific property will be a good investment also depends on the rental income it will generate, as well as the ongoing costs of maintenance, repairs, and capital improvements.

QUICK TIP

Tax Benefits

Rental properties have some tax advantages over owner-occupied properties. What you spend on upkeep and repairs for a rental property is generally tax deductible. You also get a break for depreciation, which is an allowance for the wear and tear over time on your property. This gives you an added tax write-off without any money leaving your pocket. You also write off the money you pay for the mortgage, offset by the income you receive. Consider these factors when deciding whether buying rental property is the right move for you.

What makes for a good investment?

If you were shopping for a home of your own, you'd define your dream place by listing everything you wanted and needed in your ideal property. Deciding on the characteristics of a good rental property requires a different mindset. Your criteria for determining which rental property to purchase will have nothing to do with *your* wants and needs: you aren't going to be living there. What matters is what your potential tenants will think. Unless you can successfully figure out what the rental market is looking for—and how to price it right—you probably won't reach your investment goals.

A number of key attributes should be considered when you're looking at residential rental properties:

- **Good location.** In this respect, you're looking for exactly the same sorts of things you would seek if buying a place to live yourself. Would tenants want to live here? What's the character of the neighborhood? Is it safe? What's the quality of the local school system?

  A property in a good location is likely to appreciate more in good markets and hold its value during downtimes. You'll also be able to charge higher rents for a property in a desirable neighborhood.

- **Reasonable condition.** Unless you're a dedicated repair person—and have enough time to be on call when things go wrong— purchase property that's already in good shape. Then you won't need to be constantly on the alert to keep the plumbing going, the appliances working, or the roof from leaking. Choosing a low-maintenance property will help you maintain a manageable stress level.

INSIDER'S INSIGHT

Look for High-Turnover Locations

"*Make sure the rental property is in a location where there's a relatively high degree of transient activity. Properties near a college or university, or in a city center where a lot of young people move after graduating, are prime areas for rentals.*"

Noah Seidenberg,
Agent, Coldwell Banker,
Evanston, Illinois

INSIDER'S INSIGHT

Consult Fellow Landlords

"Your very first step should be to call local landlords and ask them about the conditions of the market, including the rental prices as well as the typical damage deposit and other terms of the area's standard contracts. Most will be happy to help."

Brad Weber, Realtor and Broker, AA Realty, Eagan, Minnesota

■ **Profitable rental history.** You'll want a property that attracts long-term tenants who pay their rent promptly. You'll also want a location with high occupancy rates, whether you're buying a single-family or a multi-unit dwelling. If you live in an area with rent-control laws, investigate which units are controlled and how that will affect your cash flow. To calculate a rental property's potential cash flow, go to *http://homebuying.about.com* and click on the calculator.

QUICK TIP

Get Rich Quick?

Type "real estate investment" into any search engine and you'll get a host of schemes that promise to deliver huge—and immediate—returns on real estate investments. These range from property offers in locations that are supposedly filled with fast-to-appreciate bargains to "zero down payment" strategies for securing financing for rental properties. There are also numerous seminars, courses, and books that claim to unlock the secrets of real estate investment. Don't trust them. It's true that some people have had the savvy—and the luck—to make money in the real estate market. But for the most part, they spend their time concentrating on their core real estate business, rather than giving seminars. Check with the Better Business Bureau before committing money to such schemes.

CHAPTER 37

Make the Offer and Secure Financing

Calculate cash flow and overall profitability

O ne of the most important things you can do when considering a rental property is to estimate how much cash will be coming in and how much will be going out. That will give you the overall cash flow you can expect. You will learn: 1) whether you can afford to manage the property in question and 2) whether it will ultimately be profitable for you. This distinction is important: an investment could be a good one in the long term, but if the rental income doesn't cover the expense of maintaining the property—and your cash resources are limited—you should pass on the opportunity.

QUICK TIP

Tax Alert

The U.S. government gives homeowners a tax break on the profits when they sell an owner-occupied home. These tax breaks are not available for income property. When you sell income property, you will pay tax on any profit—or have to find another investment property.

Figuring out whether you can afford the operating costs of a property is a relatively simple calculation. First you add up the annual rent you expect—factoring in the possibility that you might experience some vacancies. Then you subtract your annual mortgage payments (principal and interest) and your operating expenses (utilities, insurance, property taxes, ongoing maintenance and repairs). You'll come up with a basic cash flow calculation that tells you approximately how much inflow (or outflow) of cash you can expect.

Cash Flow Calculation

Rental Income
(Multiply monthly rental payments by 12, then subtract at least 5 percent of the total to allow for months when the property might be vacant)

MINUS

Annual mortgage payments
(Include principal and interest)

MINUS

Operating expenses
(Any expenditure that involves paying for any aspect of running the property. This includes property tax payments; annual insurance premiums, including property, fire, and liability; utilities; and ongoing maintenance and repairs. After summing up all estimates, add another 10 percent of the total to cover unanticipated maintenance.)

TOTAL

Determining whether you can operate the property for an overall annual loss or profit is a bit more complicated. Your first step is to figure out the *taxable* revenue you'll get from the property. This figure is calculated by adding up all the rental income, then subtracting operating expenses (as above), your mortgage *interest* (not including the principal), and depreciation.

Depreciation is the amount you can subtract from your rental income every year to cover the inevitable wear and tear and overall deterioration of a building. Calculate depreciation by taking the appraised value of the property (your lender will insist on having the market value set by a professional appraiser) and dividing it by 27.5 years, which is the legal amount of time over which you are allowed to depreciate such property. If you purchased an apartment building for $500,000, your annual depreciation would be $18,182.

Rental Profit/Loss

Rental Income

MINUS

Operating Expenses
(Note: This does not include major renovations or repairs such as replacing the roof or the plumbing system or building a new addition.)

MINUS

Mortgage Interest

MINUS

Depreciation

PROFIT/LOSS   **TOTAL**

You may well come up with a taxable *loss* for the property even if you have positive cash flow.

Loss of Liquidity

Whether you're buying a place to rent or a place of your own, you need to calculate how much cash you'll need to cover all the costs involved. The price of owning any property includes the expense of the monthly mortgage and funds for property taxes, insurance, utilities, and routine upkeep, as well as major—and often unexpected—repairs and renovations. These costs increase for rental property, because of the bigger down payment that is generally required and the higher interest rate that lenders will generally charge for your loan.

Lenders also require you to have significant reserve funds in the bank before they will agree to give you a mortgage. And if you are counting on the rental income to pay most of your operating expenses, you will need to take into account the likelihood of vacancies that will eat into your cash flow. Even if you are able to get a new tenant as soon as an existing one leaves, you'll generally lose two weeks to a month's rent as you paint, clean carpets, and freshen up the property before the new tenant moves in. You'll typically need substantially more cash to invest in rental property than you would for a home of your own.

The IRS rules regarding rental property deductions are constantly evolving, so it is very important to get advice from a tax professional! In general, if you are managing the property yourself, you can deduct rental losses from your regular income. It can actually be a good thing to have a net loss on a property, as long as your cash flow is positive or close to break-even. That's because of the tax break involved (see page 186). All of this has nothing to do with the intrinsic value of the property. If you have chosen wisely, the value will increase over time, as will your share of equity, as you pay off your mortgage.

Financing

A stellar credit report is essential for securing financing for an investment property. The requirements for qualifying for this kind of financing are more rigorous than those for buying a home you'll live in, so you'll need a larger down payment and you'll pay higher interest rates to qualify for a loan. Lenders typically expect down payments of 20 to 25 percent for rental property. But some want as much as 40 percent down. And interest rates for rental properties are sometimes as much as 2 percentage points higher than for a home you'd buy to live in yourself.

The lender will likely also require that you have fairly substantial cash reserves after the deal has closed. This is because of the risk of vacancies, unanticipated repairs, and the need to cover general operating expenses to keep your property up to a livable standard for tenants. These cash reserves can be as much as six months' worth of the expenses of running the property.

So keep in mind that even if the *price* of a rental property is less than that of a home you'd occupy yourself, your actual *costs* and out-of-pocket expenditures may be much higher.

Before You Make an Offer

Never take the seller's word for anything. In addition to getting everything in writing, request official documentation of a number of key aspects of the property:

- **Determine the legality of the units.** The seller should provide documentation establishing the legality of all units, as well as their compliance with zoning laws and building codes.

- **Get copies of all licenses.** Licenses might be necessary in order to rent out the property. Check with local and state government agencies, and get copies of all necessary permits from the current owner.

- **Ask for all tax bills.** Depending on where the property is located, local or regional rental taxes might be levied on your rental income. Get copies of all tax bills and evidence that they've been paid.

- **Examine rental contracts and other tenant-related documents.** Never make an offer to purchase a property until you have copies of all forms that completely document the rental terms of current tenants, as well as rents being charged.

- **Acquire all financial records.** So you can properly estimate cash flow and operating loss or expense, the current owner should give you financial records that document annual income and expenses for the preceding 12 to 18 months.

- **Obtain estoppel certificates.** An estoppel certificate is a legal document sometimes required by lenders. Renters must sign it to verify the major points of the rental contract (the rent, the contract timeframe, and the terms, for example) that exist between the current owner and the tenant.

Being a Landlord

ven if owning rental property makes good financial sense, there are ongoing management demands to consider. Whether you own commercial or residential property, you have legal—and ethical—responsibilities to your tenants. After all, they're depending on you to guarantee that they'll be able to live and/or work comfortably in the space. So although you will almost certainly be motivated to maintain the property for your own personal investment reasons, you also have the safety of your tenants and the success of their professional lives in your hands. There are a host of things you need to consider if you want to do the job right. You can hire a property management company to do the work for you (see page 197). But if you decide to go it alone, there are a number of things you need to accomplish.

■ **Find good tenants.** This is one of the keys to keeping your stress levels manageable and maintaining the value of your property. A good tenant will pay the rent on time, take care of the space, get along with the

QUICK TIP

Pets Allowed?

Some landlords refuse to allow pets because of the perceived wear and tear on property. Others allow pets (because pet owners are often stable tenants) but require an additional damage deposit or slightly increased rent. Whatever you decide, make sure the rules for pet owners are spelled out in the rental agreement.

neighbors, and not bother you with trivial issues. Good tenants who stay a long time are a bonus. It's time consuming and expensive to search for and qualify tenants.

■ **Keep your tenants happy.** Once you find good tenants, you'll want them to stay. Do this by attending to their needs without interfering with their lives (assuming that they follow the rules laid out in the contract). From the tenant's point of view, being a good landlord involves being responsive to any problems that arise—glitches in the plumbing or a broken door lock—as well as respecting their privacy.

■ **Stay on top of property upkeep.** Pay attention to the smaller details of maintenance, as well as the larger ones. Otherwise, the condition of the property will deteriorate and you'll have trouble attracting good, long-term tenants and charging the optimal amount of rent. This means painting the interior of the property every three to four years, cleaning carpets at least annually, and either paying for ongoing landscaping services or putting a clause in the rental contract that the tenant is responsible for maintaining the lawn and garden.

■ **Set a reasonable rent.** You'll want to maximize the profit from your investment without pricing yourself out of the market and taking the risk that your property will be vacant for long periods. Your best guideline for setting a reasonable rent is what the market currently bears. Check the newspapers and online rental boards to find rental rates for similar properties in your area. You may adjust your price for special benefits or drawbacks: Is your property on a noisy road? Has it been renovated recently?

■ **Draw up a detailed rental contract.** This document establishes the rights and responsibilities of both the tenant and the landlord. At minimum, the rental agreement specifies the amount of rent, the duration of the lease, the security deposit, whether pets are allowed, the specific number of tenants who will occupy the property, and any other restrictions or conditions that either party needs to fulfill. Keep in mind that each state, or even county or city, has specific laws and regulations about tenant and landlord rights. These must be incorporated into the contract. Consult an attorney to understand the particular legal aspects of rental agreements for your geographic region, rather than relying on a standard form provided by a book or from the Internet.

Commercial Rentals

Determining the price to charge for a commercial space is a bit different than figuring out what to charge for a residential property. Although prices are based primarily on the prevailing market rate per square foot, some standard procedures for commercial leases complicate matters:

- **Measure square footage accurately.** Because most leases are based on the physical dimensions of the space, the way you measure the premises is critical. It might be counterintuitive—and potentially unethical—but some landlords of commercial properties actually measure square footage from the *outside* walls. Be very clear when talking to potential tenants how you calculated the size of the space.

- **Specify extra costs, such as insurance, taxes, maintenance, and utilities.** It's not uncommon for commercial landlords to charge for—or require—special insurance or to ask tenants to pay local or regional taxes or to underwrite the costs of routine maintenance of the building, such as janitorial services. The lease you draw up should be absolutely clear about the *total* costs the tenant will pay for occupying the premises.

- **Clarify the conditions under which modifications can be made to the property.** It is not uncommon for a commercial tenant to want to make substantial changes to the premises in order to accommodate their particular business needs. A retail store tenant might want to put in walls to create a dressing room area or a manufacturer might want to add a loading dock. The precise conditions and costs involved in allowing any modifications must be specified in writing before the lease is signed.

- **Identify spaces to be shared with other tenants.** In commercial buildings, there are frequently areas that all tenants have equal rights to use. These typically include the entrance lobby and the bathrooms but can also include common reception areas, balconies, lunchrooms, patio areas, or workout facilities. The terms of use should be carefully laid out, and you'll need to decide whether it makes sense to charge extra for use of these areas above and beyond the basic rent.

- **Decide whether you want to charge "percentage rent."** Retail leases in particular can contain special clauses that give the landlord a share of the tenant's profits in addition to the rent. Whether you do this will depend entirely on local practices and what the market can bear. In prime business locations, you may derive significant revenues above and beyond the rent through this kind of profit sharing.

Find good tenants

Finding good tenants is key to your success as a landlord. It isn't always obvious from simply meeting someone whether they will pay the rent on time or treat your property with respect. Other verification is essential. For the most complete information, use *all* of these resources:

- **Credit checks.** Get the prospective tenant's name, social security number, date of birth, and signature on a form that says you have permission to seek their credit report. Many landlords charge the prospective tenant the cost of running the check. Under no circumstances should you rent to someone with a spotty credit history. If someone refuses to allow you to run a credit check, consider that a red flag and move on to the next tenant application.

Using a Property Management Firm

One alternative to managing a property yourself is to hire a property management firm. Depending on your contract, a management firm can do everything from finding and vetting tenants to collecting rent to handling all routine upkeep and repairs. Under most property management agreements, you'll only get a call when something serious requires your attention and/or involves an outlay of extraordinary expense. Keep in mind that a property management company generally takes 10 percent of the rental income off the top. And that can wipe out your operating cash, as well as any profits you'd hoped to realize from the property.

■ **Personal references.** Ask for at least two personal references—local, if possible—and then call them to make sure the prospective tenants are responsible people.

■ **Professional references.** Speak with current employers to verify that the prospective tenants are employed and that they are being paid the salary they claimed on their rental application.

■ **Previous landlords.** No one has better information about a tenant than a previous landlord. Ask if they paid their rent on time, damaged the property, disturbed the neighbors, or caused other problems.

When tenants go bad

Almost every landlord has at least one horror story about tenants who turned out to be very bad bets. Bad ones might vandalize the property, pay the rent late (or not at all), play loud music that disturbs the neighbors, or violate codes in commercial areas.

If you ever face the unpleasant task of having to evict a tenant, don't race to court right away. First, try other avenues. Eviction procedures are lengthy and costly, and they up the ante on ill will between you and your tenants. The last thing you want is for the people in possession of your valuable investment to be motivated to damage it.

Processes for dealing with disruptive tenants vary from locale to locale. Many communities have not-for-profit agencies that will attempt to mediate landlord-tenant disputes out of court. Although not legally binding—either party can walk away from negotiations without penalty—talking in the presence of an independent third party can sometimes resolve difficult situations.

Another alternative is to pay off your tenant. That's right—give them cash in exchange for their agreement to vacate the property. In such cases, never hand over the money until they are physically off the premises—and you've changed the locks.

Minimize Vacancy Rates

One of the major risks of purchasing investment property is the chance that you'll experience periods when the property is vacant. This can result in significant loss of the income you require to meet your operating costs. Although high vacancy rates can be the result of poor maintenance or improper rent levels, some aspects of the rental process are out of your control. Tenants may be transferred or laid off and will need to move immediately. They might give adequate notice, but you could still have trouble finding a suitable new tenant who can move in at the right time. You may need to do maintenance on the property that can be done only when it is vacant. To maximize the time your property is occupied:

- Insist that your tenants provide you with a *minimum* of a month's notice before vacating the property. State in your rental agreement that if they move out before that month has elapsed, they are responsible for paying rent for the entire 30-day period.

- Post a vacancy as soon as your tenants give notice. Remember, any new tenants will probably also have to give a month's notice to *their* current landlords.

- Be creative about your search. Post the vacancy everywhere you can think of: in the local newspaper, in online classifieds such as Craigslist, on community bulletin boards, or at the supermarket or town center. And don't forget to put a "for rent" sign on the front lawn!

- In really tough markets, making special concessions can help. Some landlords will offer reduced rent for the first one or two months. Others will pay for utilities, throw in a landscaping service, or include other freebies that will attract prospective tenants.

If all else fails

Sometimes you have no choice. You've exhausted every other means—discussions, mediation, pleading—and your tenants are still causing trouble or refusing to pay their rent. Some basic steps you should take before beginning eviction proceedings:

■ **Prepare the paperwork.** One of the main things a court will require is your full documentation of the reason why you are attempting to evict the tenant. It's essential to be fully prepared to defend your case with signed and dated documentation. The papers you need include the original rental application, the rental contract, and a carefully maintained list—with dates and witness names if appropriate—of all the incidents that prompted the eviction proceedings.

■ **Deliver the eviction notice.** Write down precisely why you are evicting the tenants and specify a date when you want them out of the property. The exact amount of notice required varies from state to state—it's usually 30 days—but it can be shorter. Although not required, it can be helpful to include copies of all the evidence against the tenant—for instance, copies of police reports resulting from neighbor noise complaints—to make the notice more compelling. If you are mailing the notice, make sure that you request a signed receipt. If you are delivering the notice in person, take a witness with you. If the relationship has become extremely volatile and you are fearful of your personal safety, ask to be accompanied by a police officer.

■ **Document damage to the property.** Even after an eviction, tenants can demand that they get their damage deposit back unless you've documented—and in many locales, presented them with a list of—all the damage they've caused to the property. As soon as possible after the eviction notice has been served, do a thorough inspection of the property. Take photographs of any damage. Write up a report explaining precisely the cost of making any repairs, including copies of the photographs, and present the report to your tenants. In many states, failure to provide tenants with the opportunity to dispute damages means that they get their damage deposit back in full.

Index

L

landlords
    live-in, 183, 184
    responsibilities, 194–201
lawyers, 43, 164, 172
lead paint, 155
lead pipes, 155, 159
libraries, 24, 28
liens, 142, 164, 165
loan documents, 172–73
loan origination fees, 166
location, 16–31. *See also* neighborhoods
    ideal neighborhood, 18–23
    importance of, 6
    of rental properties, 187
loss before closing, 131
lowball offers, 124

M

mandatory arbitration, 69
margin, 54, 57
microclimates, 21
model homes, 110
mortgage brokers, 48, 58–59
    ethics, 68–69
    referrals from real estate agents, 56
mortgage calculators, 10
mortgage insurance, 167. *See also* private mortgage insurance (PMI)
mortgages, 48–69
    adjustable rate (ARMs), 53–54, 57, 73
    applying for, 49, 51
    balloon, 55
    documents signed at closing, 172–73
    fees paid outside closing, 68
    fixed rate (FRMs), 53, 57, 63
    hybrid, 55, 57
    interest is tax-deductible, 4, 5
    interest-only, 55
    length, 50, 53–58
    negative amortization loans, 56
    prepayment penalties, 68
    prequalifying, 8, 51–52
    private mortgage insurance (PMI), 60, 61

Y

Yahoo! Real Estate, 28, 81
yield spread premiums, 68

Z

Zillow, 81, 125–26
zoning laws, 21, 22, 25

Acknowledgments

The Planning Shop would like to thank the staff of the Council of Better Business Bureaus and members of local Better Business Bureaus for their invaluable assistance:

- Steven Cole, President, Council of Better Business Bureaus
- Steve Cox, Vice President of Communications, Council of Better Business Bureaus
- Sheila Adkins, Director, Public Affairs
- Ron Berry, Senior Vice President, Bureau Services Division
- Steve Salter, Vice President, BBBOnLine
- Sally Munn, Vice President, Marketing & Membership Development
- Fred Elsberry, President & CEO, BBB of Metro Atlanta, Athens, and Northeast
- Gary Almond, General Manager, BBB of Los Angeles County, Orange County, Riverside County, and San Bernardino County
- Tim Johnston, President & CEO, BBB of Northern Nevada
- Tricia Rossi, Operations Manager, BBB of Eastern Massachusetts, Maine, and Vermont
- Matthew Felling, President & CEO, BBB of Central and Northern Arizona
- James Baumhart, President & CEO, BBB of Chicago and Northern Illinois
- Kip Morse, President & General Manager, BBB of Central Ohio
- Katie Young, Director of Marketing & Communications, BBB of Alaska, Oregon, and Western Washington
- Charlie Mattingly, President & CEO, BBB of Louisville, Kentucky

Alice LaPlante would like to thank the following for their insight and expertise:

- Lovinda Beal, Realtor, Cornish & Carey, Portola Valley, California
- Scott Brader, Branch Manager, Colony Mortgage, Westerville, Ohio
- Nancy Bristow, Realtor, Emerald Coast Realty, Pensacola, Florida
- Mike Dawson, Broker, RealCo, Fresno, California
- Kenneth Etter, Broker, Kenneth Etter Realty, Reno, Nevada
- Maggie Griffin, Realtor, Weichert Realtors, Wallingford, Connecticut
- Richard Harmon, Home Inspector, RMH & Associates, Cleveland, Ohio
- Joe Loparo, Realtor, Gallagher & Lindsey, Alameda, California
- Gary Love, Realtor, Realty South, Birmingham, Alabama
- Pat Perelli, Realtor, John Hall & Associates, Phoenix, Arizona
- Noah Seidenberg, Agent, Coldwell Banker, Evanston, Illinois
- Cristy Shaw, Broker associate, Keller Williams Realty, Orange Beach, Alabama
- Sam Silver, Realtor, VIP Properties, Valencia, California
- J.D. Songstad, Realtor, RE/Max Westside Properties, Los Angeles, California
- Brad Weber, Realtor and Broker, AA Realty, Eagan, Minnesota

Every member of The Planning Shop's extended team is dedicated to producing the highest quality products and brings a special talent that enables us to develop thorough, practical, helpful, and graphically appealing books and business tools:

- Rhonda Abrams, Founder and CEO
- Maggie Canon, Managing Editor
- Mireille Majoor, Editorial Project Manager
- Deborah Kaye, Director of Academic Sales
- Rosa Whitten, Office Manager
- Diana Van Winkle, Graphic Designer
- Alice LaPlante, Writer
- Kathryn Dean, Copyeditor
- Lloyd Davis, Proofreader and Indexer
- Bridgett Novak, Contributing Editor
- Arthur Wait, Design and Technology Consultant
- Cosmo, Chief Canine Companion

The latest business tips, trends, and insights...

...all in The Planning Shop's free monthly email newsletter!

Want to stay on top of the latest trends in marketing, sales, and management? Looking for tips and advice that make you more effective, competitive, and profitable? Check out The Planning Shop Report, a free email newsletter from Rhonda Abrams and The Planning Shop.

Sign up for *free* at
www.PlanningShop.com